pace yourself

How to Have Energy
in an Exhausting World

pace
yourself

Amy Arthur

DIVERSION
BOOKS

NEW YORK

Diversion Books
A division of Diversion Publishing Corp.
www.diversionbooks.com

Diversion Books and colophon are registered trademarks of Diversion Publishing Corp.

For more information, email info@diversionbooks.com.

First Diversion Books Edition: March 2024
ISBN 978-1-63576-956-2
e-ISBN 978-1-63576-924-1

Book design by Aubrey Khan, Neuwirth & Associates, Inc.

Printed in the United States of America
10 9 8 7 6 5 4 3 2 1

Diversion books are available at special discounts for bulk purchases in the US by corporations, institutions, and other organizations. For more information, please contact admin@diversionbooks.com.

The publisher does not have any control over and does not assume any responsibility for author or third-party websites or their content.

The information in this book is not a replacement for medical advice. Ask your GP before making any radical changes to your lifestyle or diet. If you know or suspect that you have a health problem, it is recommended that you seek your GP's advice. All efforts have been made to ensure the accuracy of the information contained in this book as of the date of publication. The author and publisher shall have no liability or responsibility to any person or entity regarding any loss, damage or injury incurred, or alleged to have incurred, directly or indirectly, by the information contained in this book.

For my Grandma

Contents

~~~~~~~~~

part one
Define

part two
Assess

part three
Design

Preface

One morning in 2021, I woke up unable to move. My legs burned as if I'd run a marathon in the night, and my arms were numb, my fingers tingling. Every limb felt heavy, pulled down by something much stronger than gravity.

I knew almost immediately that I was experiencing a relapse of the condition I'd had since I was fifteen years old. Myalgic encephalomyelitis, also known as chronic fatigue syndrome, has no known cause, but many develop the condition following a viral or bacterial infection. My own came on after a kidney infection that put me in the children's hospital. It has been suggested that the post-viral condition that follows COVID-19 in some people is another form of ME/CFS. Some of those with ME/CFS are thought to have fallen ill due to a problem with their immune system or an imbalance of hormones. Trauma has also been suggested as a trigger for the condition.

Despite being quite ill as a teen, I had managed my condition successfully through college and then university. At some point I began to think of myself as all but recovered. I got my dream job. I was at the start of what I hoped would be a long, successful career in journalism and science writing. And I did what everyone does when they have one foot in the door: I said yes to everything it would take to get welcomed inside.

I worked hard, putting in the hours and then some. I networked in the evenings. I used social media to connect with people who'd managed to get to where I wanted to go. If there was an opportunity,

I took it. And I loved every minute. I've always been what some might call a "workaholic," but I did—and still do—enjoy working as much as I enjoy other elements of my life.

The day before my relapse, I'd worked late covering a new COVID-19 variant. My editor wanted a piece that explained how the United Kingdom's current vaccines would fare against the new strain, and I remember him saying to me at five o'clock that day, "You can finish for today if you want. The piece can wait until tomorrow." But I didn't want to wait; I wanted to see it through and feel the satisfaction of logging off knowing I'd produced something whole, finished, good.

I had those feelings when I finally left my computer that evening. My then boyfriend (now husband) cooked us a meal, and I think we watched something on Netflix before I decided to turn in early. I went to bed feeling normal, but I woke up feeling far from it.

As many people with ME/CFS and what's now known as long COVID have experienced, the doctors who met with me weren't of much use. The offerings are slim: something to help you sleep, vitamins if you're deficient, a referral to a specialist who might take years to come to fruition. The leaflets I was given on "energy and activity management" were only slightly different from the ones I'd been offered over ten years earlier when I was first diagnosed.

Most are told, "Learn to pace yourself," but this is much easier said than done. In the ten-minute phone calls I had with my doctor, I was advised to limit my activity and prioritize rest. How would that stop the pain? The awful thoughts? The debilitating fatigue?

As a science journalist, I'm used to digging through research papers to try to find answers to seemingly unanswerable questions. If I was to learn to pace myself, I would do it with the support of physiologists, psychologists, nutritionists, sleep experts, and more. This book is the result of my desperate search for a clear and accessible approach to pacing, and evidence of my success, given that I've worked full-time to write it only two years since waking up that morning with no energy.

All of the information and advice I've included in this book are based on my own personal experiences, as well as my own research and interviews conducted with experts. But I am not a medical professional. This book is not intended to be a substitute for the advice of a doctor, and it is advised that anyone who has been feeling low on energy or fatigued for a few weeks or more visit their general practitioner.

There are so many reasons a person might feel tired. Fatigue is a common symptom of cancer, diabetes, depression, endometriosis, thyroid disorder, and heart disease. There are conditions that disrupt sleep like respiratory diseases, sleep apnea, and dementia. People who are pregnant often have trouble sleeping and experience daytime fatigue. And, of course, parenting leads to many sleepless nights. Intense stress, anxiety, burnout, excessive drug or alcohol use, shift work . . . feelings of fatigue are so common and the consequences so underappreciated.

When you're fatigued, your whole world is affected. Sometimes it appears as a weakness in the body, so that every movement is difficult and tasks you once completed with ease now take tremendous effort. Sometimes it's felt as apathy, a struggle for enjoyment or enthusiasm or even the motivation to get out of bed in the morning for another day of tiring work with no tangible reward.

In the past, I've struggled when I've heard healthy people complain about being tired. It felt like listening to rich people complain about the cost of something. But I've come to see just how pervasive feelings of fatigue are and how detrimental they can be to a person's life. It doesn't matter whether one person is more tired than another, or has more claim to the descriptor "fatigued." What matters is how we can all move forward, at a pace that is more sustainable.

I want to thank Dr. Ellen Goudsmit, who was the first to introduce pacing to the scientific understanding of ME/CFS. Dr. Goudsmit has been a lifelong champion for those with ME/CFS, holding steadfast in the face of the stigma that surrounds the condition and the questionable research methods that have sometimes been used in its study. Her work, which includes not just pacing but also premenstrual disorders, depression, cancer, and more, has changed lives. Without her, I would not have written this book.

Pacing isn't a cure for ME/CFS, cancer, or any of the aforementioned illnesses. It isn't a substitute for medication. Learning to pace yourself doesn't make all the stressors in your life magically disappear. There are problems with work culture and income and health disparities that cannot be rectified at the individual level. I do believe, however, that there is a power in the feeling of agency, in exerting what little control people have to manage their energy levels.

Social scientists talk about behavior momentum, the idea that one single behavioral change can lead to more, larger in size and impact. We also know that behaviors are contagious. We learn from one another, and we fall into habits that we see others making. Perhaps, if I show just one person how to design a better pace of life, that person will show another, and so on, until we are all a little less tired. I hope I can show you that it's possible, even if the world around you remains largely unchanged, to go at your own pace within it.

Introduction

Are You Really Alive?

Scientists are endlessly fascinated by energy and fatigue. Nutritionists evaluate the calories we get from food; sports scientists want to know how we can push our muscles past the point of fatigue; psychologists ask why certain mental states make us feel we have energy (like excitement) and others make us lethargic (like boredom). I've read research papers and spoken to experts from many different fields about how we measure levels of energy and fatigue. Yet one particular study stands out simply for its frankness.

In 1998, the World Health Organization published its tool for assessing a person's quality of life. The survey was concerned with people's perception of the life they led; how their way of living day-to-day compared to their long-term goals, what expectations they had for the future, their standards and value systems, as well as any concerns they had. It consisted of a hundred questions (enough to make people wonder how their life choices had led them voluntarily to agree to such an undertaking) and is still used in an abbreviated form today to assess quality of life around the world.

One section of the survey covers energy and fatigue and is designed to find out "how much energy, enthusiasm and endurance a person has" for daily living. This may be anywhere on a spectrum from "reports of disabling tiredness to adequate levels of energy to feeling really alive," the 1998 WHO publication reads.[1]

Is that what having energy feels like? Are you only "really alive" if you're full of vigor? We do, I suppose, refer to people as being in a zombielike state if they stagger around on minimal amounts of sleep. Bungee jumpers and skydivers might say they've never felt more alive than when they're suspended in the sky, and it's the flood of adrenaline in their system that raises the heart rate and triggers the release of sugar into the blood, making them feel like they have more energy than before.

I have struggled with my energy levels since I was fifteen. Have I not been "really alive" for more than a decade? There are definitely times when I've felt like I'm sleepwalking or on autopilot, using my energy on things I cared less and less for: working, cooking, cleaning—even socializing became a drain. But that was just how life was sometimes, wasn't it? Everyone around me seemed to be in the same capsizing boat, throwing bucketfuls of energy at everything that came their way just so they could stay afloat for another day. But while we've been busy saving ourselves from sinking in life, we've not only been carried down a channel not of our choosing, but we've also missed most of the journey.

. . .

There's a concept in sports science called teleoanticipation. *Telos* is the Greek for "end," so teleoanticipation is our brain's ability to anticipate the end point of a given exercise. For example, running a marathon takes sustained effort, and we can't just run as fast as we can and expect to keep up that pace all the way to the end. So, our brain has a way of anticipating how much energy we will need to use over the course of the exercise, to make sure we don't overdo ourselves before the finish line is in our sights. It's thought that this ability lies somewhere in the motor cortex,[2] the area of the brain responsible for planning and executing our movements.

Teleoanticipation is believed to be entirely unconscious. The brain uses knowledge from previous, similar exercises (remembering the half-marathon where you got the stitch, or the cross-country event where you overestimated your abilities and were disappointingly slow) as well as the real-time monitoring of your body. Your heart rate, breathing, blood lactate levels, muscle condition, and body temperature all feed back into your brain's calculation, which it uses to set a sustainable pace for your run.[3]

Of course, the brain isn't infallible, and we're not bound by its decisions. Some endurance runners keep a little in reserve so that they can sprint the last kilometer, although studies are unclear as to whether this helps or hinders a person's finish time. Pacing, from a runner's perspective—and I'm not speaking from experience here, as I haven't run anywhere since physical education classes in school—is teleoanticipation in practice. When runners work out their pacing for a particular race, they calculate how fast they can run without getting fatigued to the point of having to stop (hitting the wall, in runner-speak) before the end.

The pacing that I want to introduce you to in this book is a little different from that of the endurance runner. It was taught to me when I was diagnosed with ME/CFS at fifteen years old, a condition that is hallmarked by its persistent and often disabling fatigue. Pacing, I was told, is an energy management technique used to find balance between activity and rest. This balance would be unique to me, allowing me to use what energy I did have to do the things I wanted (and needed) to, so that the end of each day was marked not by debilitating pain and fatigue, but the satisfying, "normal" kind of tired you feel after a day well-lived. Pacing was recommended for people recovering from surgery long before it was used in the management of ME/CFS, and it's also taught to people with chronic pain, fibromyalgia, long COVID, and cancer.

Since my diagnosis, I've accumulated every bit of information on energy and fatigue I can possibly find, trying to figure out how I can have the kind of life I want with an energy-limiting condition. I've tried out hacks purported to save energy, boost energy, reduce fatigue, and help you sleep. I've read books on health, diet, exercise, stress, sleep, rest, and more.

I've spent nearly half my life learning how to be more aware of my energy levels, and watching how others manage theirs. If there's one thing that's clear, it's this: We humans are not very good at pacing ourselves. And I think teleoanticipation is to blame.

• • •

Imagine, for a moment, that your life is a race—not against other people, but to a finish line that you have chosen. What awaits you there?

You might find it hard to think of just one end point. I do. I want several things in life: to publish this book, to have somewhere nice to call home, to have loving family and friends around me. The analogy of life as a race falls apart quite quickly when you have more than one goal. It's like life is actually a triathlon, except you're trying to reach the finish lines for running, cycling, and swimming all at the same time. Throw in some hurdles and the keen eye of everyone around you, and the metaphor feels a bit more appropriate.

The Boom-and-Bust Pattern

Our brain's tendency for teleoanticipation is our downfall, because it makes us set arbitrary end points in life, when in reality there is no real finish line—other than the obvious one. We strive for "success" as if it is a fixed end point that we can reach by careful, calculated expenditure of time and energy. Put in the hours, and you'll be rewarded. Climb the ladder, and you'll be successful. Buy a house, get married, have children. Do life right, and you'll be happy.

Our brains, fixated on whatever end points we've decided represent "success" to us, just do what they do best. They work out the pace at which we need to move, based on whatever factors we provide them with.

This has led to what's called a boom-and-bust pattern in our lives. To reach a goal, we believe we ought to push ourselves. Do whatever it takes to reach success, because the achievement, the *telos*, is worth it.

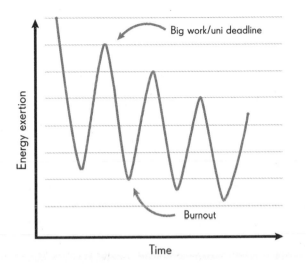

Yet once we've got the job, the book deal, the relationship, we immediately turn our minds to the next end point. Without waiting to savor the rewards of our labor, we're on to a new project, planning for the next promotion, anxious to take the next step in our relationship. You might spend nine months preparing for a new baby, but no sooner are you handed your bundle of joy than you begin to think about what's next: how and when the infant will reach "developmental milestones" like walking and talking, whether they're growing at the right pace, if your treatment now will lead the infant into a lifetime of anxious attachment and expensive therapy.

By always looking forward, you are never truly aware of what you're doing to yourself *now*. This constant use of energy without time for rest and recuperation makes up the "boom" of the cycle you likely find yourself in. It can occur in many forms, in one area of your life or in many. For people like me with health conditions that limit their energy, the temptation to use energy while you've got it is even greater, yet a boom-and-bust pattern to life is even more detrimental.

The "bust" is the crash, and it is inevitable. You cannot keep using energy and expect no repercussions. Whether you're an athlete who overtrains, a creative who claims to work best under pressure, a doctor who forgoes sleep in the name of helping more people, or someone with ME/CFS who fights against the change to their own energy . . . the "bust" will occur sooner or later. It might present as burnout or pain or a mental health condition. It may cause the end of a relationship or the loss of a job. It may be the realization that somehow you ended up in a position you never wanted to be in.

When you pace yourself, you overrule the boom-and-bust pattern of your brain's teleoanticipation. Instead of reaching for goal after goal, you focus on the balance of activity and rest that fosters good work, good health, and happiness. Your goals make up a part of your new pace, as you'll see, but they are not pursued to the detriment of everything else.

"By always looking forward, you are never truly aware of what you're doing to yourself now."

Where Does Your Brain's *Telos* Come From?

The setting of our end points, or goals as they're more commonly known, starts early. When we're young, our growth is compared against averages, our development monitored on charts. Parents, caregivers, and teachers all assess our progress through life, and when we're not meeting their expectations, they worry, fuss, or scold.

As we grow up, we start to have conversations about "what we'll do when we're older." This is our first real end point: We will be our career, and that will be that. I will be a writer. My friend will be an accountant. My brother will be a painter. We're encouraged to have just one end point, rather than several. I've worked in various industries, from customer service to marketing to journalism. When I was born, my mom worked more than one job—after her day job in sales, she went to work pulling pints at a pub—and when I left home, she was a finance manager during the week and a realtor at the weekend.

We don't tell young people this. Instead, they take on debt and stress in the pursuit of a job that can't live up to the pressure of being their life's goal.

As young adults, we also have another end point, an aesthetic one. To be attractive to others is a fluctuating, multifaceted thing, but when we're young, we place so much value on visuals. We might long to be a set weight, or have a certain amount of muscle, or clear skin, or curly hair. When we reach this end point, we think, we'll be attractive, and that will be that.

This of course is linked to another end point that many aspire to reach: a romantic relationship. I know that I put a lot of energy into reaching this particular end point, but as soon as I was (thankfully) done with dating apps, a new end point appeared. When would we move in together? Then, when would we get married? And now, we're asking ourselves, when should we start a family? After that, I expect, my end points will be in relation to my own children, starting the cycle all over again.

Having goals in life is a good thing. Goals provide us with motivation, a reason to get up in the morning. In tough times, we can console ourselves with our hopes and dreams. Purpose, according to behavioral scientist Paul Dolan, is a huge part of our overall happiness in life,[4] as important as seeking pleasure, which we can also get from achievement of our goals.[5]

But the trouble with setting ourselves these end points is that our teleoanticipatory brain uses them as the basis for our pace in life. They're the yardstick by which we measure our daily progress, and the cane by which we beat ourselves if we fall to the back of the race to achieve each one.

We like to think that our day-to-day activities are in pursuit of these end points. I write every day because I have a goal to publish a book. You might save money to put toward a deposit on a house.

In truth, these goals only really crop up when something or someone prompts us to think about them. Do you think about your career goals on a daily basis, or only when your annual review comes along? Does your community and local environment affect you every time you step out your front door, or only when you're looking for a new place to live? Sometimes, our everyday actions are in direct opposition to our goals: spending our salary on a party instead of textbooks, skipping a lecture to sleep in, choosing a self-care evening over socializing.

We set these goals with good intentions. I think that, really, we set goals because we recognize that our ultimate end point is happiness. So that when we reach the end and reflect on our time here on Earth, we can say that we did things that were good and worthwhile.

But, day-to-day, the pursuit of happiness falls by the wayside. We forget that it's joy we seek and instead make decisions based on how much money they'll bring in or save or because people around us are making those same choices or because overall happiness seems so abstract that we opt for short-term pleasures.

It seems selfish to think that I take happiness away from future-me to make current-me feel a little better. I feel guilty when I choose to act in ways that are seemingly in opposition to my goals. I am going against my brain's teleoanticipatory tendency, and the discord between the pace I think I should be moving at and the way I'm going about life feels wrong, radical even.

I'm sure you know the story of Icarus, whose father made him a pair of wings from feathers and beeswax. Icarus, in his elation, flew too high, and the sun melted his wings.

Yet in the Greek legend, Icarus was also cautioned against flying too low, for the seawater of the ocean below posed as many problems for his wings as the heat of the sun. He was to follow his father's steady path. Instead, after reaching his great height, Icarus fell to his death as his father watched.

The advice "to live between the extremes" has been repeated over the years. The philosopher Aristotle wrote that the virtues of a person's character should rest at a golden mean, with no facet in excess or deficiency. The concept of balance also appears in many religions, including the Buddha's teachings of a "middle way" between extremes and the Quran's emphasis on balance and moderation. Now, psychologists are beginning to understand how important balance and harmony are in life, referring to them as well-being's "golden thread."[6]

A New Pace of Life

At a time when busyness is seen as a symbol of status, when your sense of worth is determined by your number of side hustles or followers on social media, and everyone around you is flying toward the sun, it's very difficult to take a steady pace. You might've tried making changes already, vowing to spend more time resting or attempting to break bad habits. But change isn't easy, especially if you feel you're making it on your own.

Pace Yourself was written to give people like you everything required to design a better pace of life. It will help you gain a deeper awareness of your own feelings of energy and identify the activities (and people) that affect your energy levels, for better or for worse. The advice and research mentioned in this book should give you the confidence to set boundaries around the way your time and energy are used, and help protect your new pace of life against the pushback that naturally occurs when others notice change.

Of course, you'll never have complete authority over where your energy goes: Your work will still demand more of you, your kids will need feeding, and life will throw surprises at you, as it does. But even in these circumstances, pacing can help you hold onto what control you do have over your own mind and body. At work, you'll be aware of your own capacity and manage others' expectations accordingly, rather than agreeing to pile more onto your plate under the belief that your limited time and energy can somehow accommodate unlimited demands. When you're being pulled in all directions, by your family, your friends, your own needs and wants, pacing helps you to prioritize based on the energy you have available. It allows you to let go of the exhausting idea that you must do everything, do something, all the time. Instead, you choose to live life at a more manageable pace, and show everyone around you that it's possible to actually enjoy the here-and-now without jeopardizing the future.

In Part One, you'll learn about energy: where it comes from, what affects how much we have, and how to tell if you've reached the point of exhaustion. Feelings of energy are difficult to study, which makes it even harder for researchers to identify exactly what causes us to have energy and how we get fatigued. There are still gaps in the knowledge, questions without complete answers. This book, then, contains an overview of what is known about energy and how this can be applied to your daily life.

For ease, I've categorized the science into three types of energy: emotional, mental, and physical. Pacing involves finding a balance between these three types and the different forms of rest that allow you to recover each one. But there is a lot of crossover between activities and the types of energy; movement and exercise involves the brain, while our feelings can also present physical symptoms. The mind and body aren't separate entities, though people still talk of "mental" and "physical" health. In truth, energy is such a broad topic that it has to be simplified slightly. At the end of this first part of the book, you'll begin monitoring your own energy levels in what we call a pacing diary.

Part Two will teach you how to assess and amend your current diet, sleep, and rest activities. Meeting these needs is crucial to supporting your mind and body with energy. You'll also decide on the activities that will make up your "vital pace"—the baseline of energy expenditure that you'll use in your new pace of life. Getting this right may take a bit of trial and error, because it'll vary greatly depending on your own situation, but it's important that this amount of activity doesn't use too much or too little of each of the three types of energy. In the story of Icarus, the vital pace is the safe and steady path directly between the sun and the sea.

Of course, you'll still want to pursue goals, achievements, a social life, and happy times. There will be reasons for using up all your energy on activities, for pushing yourself when you want to. In Part Three, then, we'll look at "pacing up": increasing activity and energy use without booming and busting. Using the science of happiness, goal pursuit, and time use, you'll design a new pace that incorporates everything you've decided belongs in your life.

Each of the parts in *Pace Yourself* will contain a main task that's needed for you to begin pacing. You'll also find smaller tasks within some of the chapters of the book. These have been created to aid you in designing your new pace of life and, while optional, I do recommend you give each one a go.

> "Let go of the exhausting idea that you must
> do everything, do something, all the time."

Whether you're in a permanent state of exhaustion or just feeling like you never have quite enough energy for everything you want to do, pacing can help you take control over your own energy levels and restore balance to your life. We'll also discuss the importance of boundaries and, often, compromises. So much of our energy use is dictated by or demanded of us by others. Knowing when and how to compromise, and when to stick up for your own rest and activity, will be important in your new pace of life.

In the beginning, pacing helped me stabilize my days, gave me times of rest and recuperation that weren't marred by pain or guilt or fear of missing out. In time, I stopped making decisions based on goals someone else had set for me, instead choosing to put my energy into things that brought me happiness and a sense of achievement entirely of my own making.

Getting ill changed my pace of life irrevocably, but here I am, thirteen years later, feeling more alive than ever before.

Are you ready to live? Then let's learn to pace yourself.

pace
yourself

part one
Define

"The real price of everything, what
everything really costs to the [person]
who wants to acquire it, is the toil and
trouble of acquiring it."

—Adam Smith, *The Wealth of Nations*

IN THIS FIRST PART we'll look at the three ways your body uses energy: emotionally, mentally, and physically. We'll also learn about the signs of exhaustion in each of these three areas, and identify some restful activities that help restore our energy. At the end of this section, you'll create a pacing diary, which will help you see where your emotional, mental, and physical energy is going over the course of a week and whether there are boom-and-bust patterns in your activity.

For ease, the three types of energy have been separated into individual chapters, but in reality there is a lot of crossover between them. A task that uses a lot of mental activity may also be emotionally demanding, while a physically challenging activity will also require mental strength and resilience. Although our brains (and books) like to compartmentalize, remember that pacing is a holistic approach to our energy, and works best when we can step back and appreciate our activities as jigsaw pieces, not the whole picture of fatigue.

Remember that feeling tired is normal and useful—it's our warning sign to slow down before we do ourselves damage. Our bodies are designed to make us feel tired in the evening so that we can fall asleep and our brains can perform the housekeeping work that they can't do while we're awake. Tiredness isn't just a sign to sleep, though; it's also an indication of when we ought to rest or stop a strenuous activity. But these feelings of fatigue can grow out of control and start to affect our well-being over time. And if we ignore them for too long, it becomes difficult to see how truly pervasive they've become, and how things that once energized us are now barely stimulating.

one

Highs and Lows

~~~~~~~~~~~~~~~~~~~~~~~~~

Emotional Energy

IT MAKES SENSE to start a chapter on the way our emotions use our energy with some examples, perhaps even a list of emotions and their corresponding energy demands. Pacing ourselves would be easier if we could just refer to a compendium of emotions every time we felt something, keeping track of the energy we spend and knowing exactly how much we have left at any point.

But the way we use our energy—be it emotionally, mentally, or physically—is unique. This is because the entire experience of using energy is dependent on a whole host of factors, such as our childhood, our mindset, and our physiology. When it comes to our emotions, the amount of strain put on our mind and body is influenced by the feeling itself, but also the context, whom we're with, and how we were raised to manage emotions. Our culture also has a big impact on our emotional experiences, as does being neurodiverse.

Researchers have yet to come up with a definition for "emotion," though not for lack of trying. In the 1990s, psychologist Paul Ekman and his team were studying facial expressions when realized no one had yet established what emotions actually were.[1] They came up with a theory that said there were six core emotions: anger, disgust, fear, happiness, sadness, and surprise. All emotional feelings fell within one of these core categories, Ekman posited.

Since the 1990s, psychologists have tried to re-create Ekman's studies, or to undertake their own research to determine which emotions are innate and core to human experience. But, as Dr. Dean Burnett writes in *Emotional Ignorance: Lost and Found in the Science of Emotion*, a growing number of researchers reject the idea that there are any "basic" emotions, instead asserting that the way we feel is "made up" in the moment.[2] That our emotional experiences are vastly different, even when they could be characterized by the same emotion. Happiness in response to praise, for example, is different than the happiness we feel when we're lying in the sun, listening to the sound of the waves rolling up the beach with our favorite drink in hand.

Though in this chapter I'll refer to research that bundles up our emotions into their "basic" groups, keep in mind that your experience may vary across your daily activities.

What Is Emotional Energy?

According to neuroscientists, our emotions fall on a scale of arousal— not sexual arousal, but energetic arousal. High-arousal emotions are said to be energized states that amplify our nervous systems, while low-arousal emotions lead us to an enervated, relaxed state.[3]

Examples of high-arousal, or energetic, emotions are joy, rage, disgust, amazement, terror, vigilance, and excitement. Low-arousal emotions, or low-energy states, might be peace, boredom, trust, loneliness, misery, helplessness, and contentment.

Of course, what science says is "energetic" or "low energy" might not fit with your experience. It's also worth mentioning that studies have shown that Western, individualist cultures seem to prefer and value high-energy emotions over low-energy ones.[4] One study showed that the average American's conception of happiness relied on upbeat, high-arousal emotions, while the Chinese idea of happiness was focused on lower-energy feelings of harmony, trust, safety, and stability.[5]

The desire to feel everything strongly could be what leads some people to stress and burnout, though that's not to say those who value low-energy emotions don't suffer from these and related ailments. Nor would I say that, in pacing, the goal is to only have low-energy emotions—where would be the fun in life without joy, excitement, anger?—but instead should be to identify how your mood affects your energy and vice versa.

It's worth noticing the kinds of emotions we have on a day-to-day basis. Some people will naturally feel their emotions more than others, and emotional stability is often considered part of our personality. Some, including many neurodivergent people, will also find regulating their emotions harder than others. Stopping yourself from teetering over a low-energy emotion into a highly aroused state can sometimes feel impossible, though the practices of emotional rest that come later in this chapter should also help you find low-arousal states. Of course, these sudden, unregulated, big feelings aren't always bad, as they can bring joy and excitement and even ecstasy.

I find that high-energy emotions can do one of two things for me. Some, like excitement and joy, will make me feel like I have more energy in general. On my wedding day, I stood for pictures longer than I'd been able to for months. I spoke to everyone I could, even though conversations usually tire me out fast. I danced until the bar closed. The day after, though my feet ached and my head throbbed, I felt surprisingly okay—as I imagine most people do after their wedding.

Then there are the emotions that I know just tire me out more than others. I can get fired up while I'm debating someone, but arguments, and the anger and anxiety they stir in me, will always, *always* make me more fatigued the day after.

Low-arousal states can also affect my energy in different ways. Boredom often makes me fidgety, and I look like I have plenty of energy to use but nowhere to place it. Contentment, to me, feels like a pleasant kind of sleepiness, a desire to watch how everyone else is using their energy around me without expending any of my own.

When you complete your pacing diary in chapter 4, you'll be on the lookout for emotional energy. But it's not always easy to identify emotions, let alone the amount of energy that they take up. Many people have been taught that to show emotions is to be weak, or that by doing so you must be "hysterical," untrustworthy, or unintelligent. How do you feel about emotional distress? Have you learned that it is okay to show emotional distress, or were you taught, by your caregivers or by social media, that struggling is a sign of weakness or of being "mad"?

Noticing Emotions

If you have difficulty identifying your emotions in a certain situation, you may want to try one of the following exercises:

- Notice physical patterns. When you feel an emotional change, try writing down the sensations you feel. Is your heart racing, or is it slow and steady? Are you hot or cold, buzzing with energy or sapped of life? Are you crying or shouting? Once you've listed your physical feelings and the outward expressions of your emotion, you may find it easier to name it. Listening to your body in this way is called interoception, and it has been found to be helpful with emotional regulation.[6]
- Give it a metaphor. In her book *A Manual for Being Human*, clinical psychologist Dr. Sophie Mort says that choosing a word to label how you feel can help de-intensify your emotional experience, even if that word isn't a specific emotion—so saying "this feeling is stony in my chest" or "I feel like a firework about to go off" is just as valid as if you were to search long and hard for an emotional label.[7]
- Identify your motivation. The brain systems that look after emotion and motivation are linked,[8] meaning many of your feelings will be accompanied by the motivation to do something. Sadness might motivate you to cry, anger might result

in the urge to cause physical pain, and you might seek to extend feelings of happiness by repeating whatever action caused it in the first place. So, if you're not sure of the emotion you're feeling, ask yourself, "What am I motivated to do in this situation?"

- Eliminate what you're not feeling. Sometimes it's easier to rule out emotions than it is to pick out the exact feeling. By "checking off" in your mind the emotions that aren't at play, you may find yourself better able to understand what it is you're experiencing.

. . .

I still struggle with identifying certain emotions, but, as with everything, it gets easier with practice. Over time, you'll get better and better at understanding your feelings, and at noticing the energy they take or restore.

Signs You've Exhausted Your Emotional Energy

Experiencing fluctuating emotions is natural, and it's to be expected that you'll feel tired after an emotionally taxing day. But how do you know when your fatigue is excessive, when you're experiencing "true" emotional exhaustion?

While there are common symptoms, much of our feelings of fatigue—like our feelings of energy—come from within us and can't be compared to others. But if you feel like you're struggling to maintain positive emotions, or any emotions at all for that matter, then you may be in need of some emotional rest.

Just as we can feel tired at the height of a "boom" or in the depths of a "bust," exhaustion can come from spending too much or too little emotional energy. In chapter 4, you'll learn to monitor your energy expenditure and identify whether you're using too much or too little of any one type, but knowing the signs now can help you feel more in control of your overall fatigue.

Using Too Much Emotional Energy

Much of the research into emotional exhaustion has focused on burnout at work. A depletion of emotional energy is one of the three main symptoms of burnout and it tends to be the first warning sign that serious burnout is on the horizon, according to patient reports. This seemingly unexplained exhaustion at work grows and is eventually joined by negativity and a leaching of pleasure from all aspects of life.

Emotional exhaustion is particularly common in people whose work involves either **suppressing emotions** or **acting emotions**.

Emotional suppression involves ignoring any emotion, positive or negative, to appear emotionally neutral while at work. It's common in jobs where people need to put some emotional distance between themselves and their work, or where showing emotion might actually harm outcomes of the job. Many people working in healthcare have learned to suppress their emotions, either for fear of appearing too "upbeat" when delivering bad news, or for being too upset and seeming unprofessional or even unqualified. It's no surprise, then, that according to one scientific review, approximately one in three physicians is experiencing burnout at any given time.[9] Those with a tendency to people-please can also find themselves changing their emotions to fit in, or suppressing a natural desire to say "no" or show disapproval for something that's being asked of them.

While suppressing emotions harms well-being, Burnett writes that forcing yourself to display different emotions than the ones you're actually feeling is even worse. This is called *acting emotions*, and though it's common in TV and film, it's also widespread in retail and service jobs. Being made to give "service with a smile" no matter your real feelings can lead to high levels of stress and emotional exhaustion.[10] It's also likely that people who spend a lot of time around children—whether their own or in a work capacity—will be familiar with acting emotions. Humans have an innate desire to show children love and warmth and to shield them from pain. But hiding negative emotions affects you and those around you. Children learn emotional regulation from their parents and caregivers, which means they'll pick up on your choice to bury bad feelings rather than resolve them in a healthy manner. They may learn that negative or high-arousal emotions like anger and excitement aren't allowed, in turn using their own emotional energy to act out false emotions in front of you, their schoolteachers, and their friends.

Acting emotions is similar to neurodiverse masking, which involves suppressing natural behaviors and putting on emotions or facial expressions to appear neurotypical. Masking happens in the workplace, but also at school, within families, and around close friends. The behavior can be so deep-rooted that it even happens within your thoughts, judging feelings based on how someone else might view them.

Emotional exhaustion can also be linked to the efforts of people of color to conform to a systemically white corporate culture, which writer Chika Ekemezie says can involve dressing differently, talking in a way that feels unnatural, and switching to a persona that white people see as more likable. Called code-switching, Ekemezie writes, "for people of color, code-switching is a means of professional (and sometimes personal) survival. Though this kind of code-switching is often second nature, it can lead to emotional exhaustion and burnout."[11]

Sometimes, exhaustion comes from the excess of one emotion and the downplaying of all others. Grief is an example of this, because in mourning we tend to tell ourselves that we cannot be seen to be happy. We might even punish ourselves for feeling anything other than sadness, despite a loss being multifaceted: The relief felt when a person passes after a long period of illness can make us feel ashamed or guilty.

Time away from that emotion, and away from people whom you believe expect to see that emotion in you, can actually help in processing an emotional situation. One of the emotion regulation strategies that we use is known as *reappraisal,* which involves assessing the way we have responded emotionally to an event and deciding whether to react differently in the future. But if we never step away from the emotion itself, we can't properly know if the feeling is justified or helpful.

People with emotional exhaustion can also experience:

- Problems with executive function, like planning, following instructions, and being organized[12]
- Trouble with attention and focus, or getting distracted easily[13]
- Memory issues[14]
- Emotional outbursts or crying for no apparent reason[15]
- Abnormal reactions to situations, either through a lack of emotion or an excess
- Accidents at work or at home
- A fear of embarrassment, or a fear of going outside[16]
- Excessive worrying and anxiety
- Depression or low mood

Using Too Little Emotional Energy

There is a paradox at play when it comes to your energy: Using it can replenish it, and not using it can deplete it.

Imagine your emotional energy as a muscle. Use it too much, without respite, and it'll strain and falter. It'll be out of action for a while, but you'll be able to start training it again after it's had sufficient rest. If you don't use a muscle, however, it never learns to tolerate the stress, the energy, of exercise. It will always struggle when put under any strain, yet life will show up to put strain on it anyway.

If you never spend emotional energy, you'll find yourself fatigued by any new feeling. A small upset will wipe you out, little joys will be confusingly exhausting. This makes it even harder to use your emotional energy, because all the associations suggest feeling anything will cause fatigue. In these cases, pacing yourself toward energy expenditure is paramount. Small, managed emotions will help you establish a better relationship with your emotional energy and slowly train that muscle back up to experiencing all the benefits of its use: happiness, excitement, laughter.

Some people can generate emotions on their own, through hobbies or play or purposeful work. But when you're exhausted, seeking out these experiences usually demands more energy than you can muster. You may realize that you're lacking the deep connections that all humans need, yet the little energy you can employ might be spent seeking contact on social media, which rarely satisfies our emotional needs (more on that in chapters 7).

"There is a paradox at play when it comes to your energy: Using it can replenish it and not using it can deplete it."

If one of the most common causes of emotional inactivity is loneliness, then we should all be concerned that, according to one study conducted in 2022, 25.99 million people—that's more than the number of people living in the state of Florida—reported feeling lonely, at least occasionally.[17] Of these, 3.8 million experienced chronic loneliness.[18]

Experiencing fatigue, whether due to illness, burnout, extreme stress or life in general, can be isolating. With little energy to spare, you withdraw from everything you can. Usually, your social life is one of the first things to take a hit. You think you're protecting yourself from using excess energy on stress and anger, but without fostering positive emotions, you're going from using too much to too little emotional energy in a short space of time. Remember that the "bust" is just as damaging as the "boom."

Emotions, though, are contagious. You can catch them through meaningful relationships, and also from strangers. Finding little ways to experience positive emotion is important in building back up to a life of good energy. There will be more on this in chapter 11, but for now, consider how you can find small moments of positivity in your day.

Emotional Exhaustion in ME/CFS and Long COVID

One of the hallmarks of ME/CFS is what's called *post-exertional malaise*, or PEM. This is when activity—emotional, mental, or physical—causes a worsening of symptoms.[19] Usually, the stressor is something that would be tolerated in people without the condition, but triggers new or exacerbated symptoms in people with ME/CFS. Those with long COVID also report worsening after activity, though there are fewer published studies on PEM within this group. One paper suggests that PEM appears to be more severe in people with long COVID because the "newness" of the condition has meant patients are not properly taught how to manage energy and activity to avoid PEM.[20]

I experience PEM whenever I work too long without a break, spend too long on my feet, or during episodes of low mood. For other people my age, these things can make a person tired or feel a small amount of pain, like a headache from too much screen use or sore legs after exercise. But my PEM can be overwhelming, so much so that I can't move from my bed or the sofa, I struggle to talk and string sentences together, and feel like I might faint at any moment.

Unlike a healthy person's immediate response to overexertion, PEM tends to be delayed, appearing between twelve and forty-eight hours after the activity, and it can last for days, weeks, or even longer.

The specifics of PEM, including symptoms and onset, can vary greatly from person to person, but also depending on the type of exhaustion. My PEM is worse during physical exhaustion, though I find the effects of emotional exhaustion will last much longer. If you don't know the triggers and symptoms of your PEM, the pacing diary in chapter 4 will help you identify these experiences.

PEM and the boom-and-bust lifestyle are hugely correlated. During a boom, it's tempting to take on more activity and push yourself while your body is feeling (relatively) good. But with the bust comes PEM. This is why pacing can help reduce PEM.

Recharging Your Emotional Energy

In pacing, it's important to balance emotional activity with periods of rest and low energy. These may be times of low-arousal emotions, or they might involve activity that inspires emotions opposite to those you generally feel on a daily basis. Sometimes, activity that uses your mental or physical energy can offer respite from intense emotion. At the end of this chapter, you'll write down a list of things you can do for emotional rest, and it will be good to have a mix of low- and high-energy activities.

There are ways to minimize the effects of emotional suppression and acting, and to reduce emotional exhaustion, though it's important to note that rest alone is not a cure for the many causes of this type of fatigue. The many external factors at play here mean that it is unreasonable and even damaging to suggest that individuals are solely responsible for their emotional exhaustion. My aim is to help you use what control you have to reduce the impact of the things that are out of your control.

One way to adjust your own emotions is by **being around others** who exude the feelings you desire. This might be because they are generally low-energy people—my best friend, Emily, for example, is soft-spoken, warmhearted, and very calming to be with—or because they encourage you to stop suppressing or acting emotion. Surrounding yourself with these people is effective because, as I've mentioned, emotions are contagious: As social creatures, we are influenced by others and will naturally mimic their movements, facial expressions, and, ultimately, emotions.[21]

Undertaking **physical activity** can also boost your mood by releasing endorphins that induce feelings of pleasure in your brain. Exercise has been shown to reduce anxiety and depression, and boosts your self-esteem along with positive emotions.[22] For extra benefit, you could schedule a workout or a walk with a friend. Friends will hold you accountable and make you more likely to actually get out and about, and also make the experience enjoyable during exercise as well as after. Of course, while exercise doesn't generally demand much emotional energy, it isn't suitable as rest if you're also physically tired.

You might find that **mental challenges** can be used as a distraction, taking you out of your emotion into a place of low arousal. This is one way I deal with the overwhelming sadness I feel around a certain time of the month: I can't put my energy into solving the problem, because I'm not upset over anything in particular, so instead I try to calm my mind by distracting it. Meditation can be one form of distraction, as can playing video games or reading absorbing fiction.

If stress is one of the causes of your exhaustion, you may find it helpful to **embrace playfulness**. Play has been shown to alleviate feelings of stress, while teaching new coping mechanisms and building resilience.[23] Brené Brown, in her book *The Gifts of Imperfection*, encourages the cultivation of play in our lives as part of letting go of the "status symbol" of exhaustion and overwork.[24] It can be daunting, even embarrassing, to start thinking about how to inject more moments of play into our life. For many, the need to excel and work for acclaim has led to the point of burnout and fatigue. So, stepping into the territory of play, where all hours are non-billable, where rules are thrown out the window, and new skills start with mediocrity, takes courage. But there are all sorts of ways to play, and you might want to try some different activities before settling on the ones that you'll build into your new pace of life.

Studies have shown that belief in yourself can make you less likely to get emotionally exhausted at work, so you could try writing and reading **affirmations of ability and reminders of control**. I'm not always fond of the advice "have you tried a gratitude journal?" but there is research that supports the use of positive, emotion-focused coping strategies. In particular, when you believe that you have the ability and the agency to control outcomes in your life, you have better emotional well-being.[25] This only applies if you *can* find ways to have control and agency in life, but actually by picking up this book you have confirmed your desire and ability to change, to take control. If you're scheduling times of emotional rest into your life, that's another way you're acting with agency.

It's important that you set boundaries for when and how you'll use your emotional energy. This doesn't mean you have to have complete control over your emotions, nor does it rely on the ability to prevent any and all unexpected emotional activity. Out of the three types, emotional energy is the one that we end up having least control over. It can be taken without warning and without our say-so: sudden grief, happiness, and anger are parts of life.

You can, however, decide on limits for your emotional energy use and make a conscious effort to employ some of the rest and low-energy activities mentioned here whenever you notice that you're close to emotional exhaustion. This might mean using your child's naptime as an opportunity for your emotional rest, or switching your phone to airplane mode for a few hours to prevent any further depletion by well-meaning friends or emails designed to stir up your anger or excitement so that you'll sign a petition or make a purchase.

TASK

Come up with ten activities you could use as emotional rest. Try to get a range of solo and group activities, and a good balance of mental, physical, and low-energy ideas. These activities will be added to those you come up with in the next two chapters to form a "Rest Bank," which you'll then pull from when you design your new pace of life in chapter 13.

> "By picking up this book you have confirmed your desire and ability to change, to take control."

5 Principles of Pacing Emotional Energy

1. Emotions fall on a scale of low to high energy. Try noticing how your emotions make you feel, and whether certain ones are more tiring or more calming than others.
2. It's not always easy to know what emotions you're feeling. If you're unsure, use some of the exercises on [pages 6–7] or search online for techniques to identify emotions.
3. Emotional exhaustion has a serious impact on your health and can be a sign of impending burnout.
4. Suppressing or acting emotions can be one of the most emotionally exhausting things you have to do. Consider whether you spend a large amount of energy on suppressing or acting, and try to find healthy and safe ways to allow your true feelings out regularly.
5. Emotional rest can take many forms, and what works for one person might not work for you. Begin building your own list of emotionally restful activities so that you can later incorporate them into your new pace of life.

two

Mind Over Matter

~~~~~~

Mental Energy

IN EVERY WAKING MOMENT, our brain is processing information from the world around us and from within our bodies. Every day we have several thousand thoughts,[1] most of which pass fleetingly through our subconscious. Many of these thoughts are effortless, using little to no mental energy—musings about the weather, remembering fond times, imagining how we'd look in the new outfit we just bought, or picturing what we plan to make for our next meal.

But within each of these thoughts is the opportunity for depletion of our energy. If the National Weather Service has predicted a heat wave, our thoughts about the weather could snowball into something less innocuous; for example, concerns about our health or those around us, or perhaps the heat wave might make us worry about the threat of climate change and extreme weather events worldwide. Similarly, while we might be pleased with a new outfit bought for a special occasion or job interview, we might trigger financial worries about being able to make the next month's rent as a result of buying it. When thoughts and worries combine, they can deplete our energy by raising our heart rate and making us feel stressed.

Even now, while you're trying to read this book, something in the above paragraph might have triggered your mind to wander. Perhaps you're half-reading and half-watching your kids play, or keeping an eye on the pasta boiling on the stove. The demands for our attention are so great, we can't see any other way than to multitask, even though most of us know we'd be much more efficient if we could just focus on one thing long enough to see it through.

This mindwandering, as neuroscientists refer to the jumping from one thought to another, from past to future, imagining the real and unreal, has helped us learn and evolve.[2] We couldn't reason with one another without making appeals to past alliances, or plan for the future without the ability to predict based on previous events. But all too often our mindwandering leads to distraction, procrastination, or fatigue.

We've all experienced mental fatigue at some point in our lives—after difficult exams, a long day in front of the computer, or as a result of another condition, like depression or dementia. But we don't tend to consider our mental energy when making decisions about how we spend our days. We wouldn't plan to run a marathon every day for the next five years, no matter what title and how much money was offered to us, yet we'll exhaust our brains without question in the pursuit of our careers.

In this chapter you'll be encouraged to consider the things that demand your mental energy and whether they have to be so effortful. While too little mental stimulation has its problems, most of us are pushing our minds too far without giving ourselves opportunity for mental rest and recuperation.

"We wouldn't plan to run a marathon every day for the next five years, yet we'll exhaust our brains without question in the pursuit of our careers."

What Is Mental Energy?

What I refer to as mental energy is usually described as "cognitive effort" in scientific literature. Like emotions, the impact of mental activity on our energy levels is subjective and hard to quantify, but researchers have found some similarities in the way people seem to experience the depletion of mental energy.

Daniel Kahneman, author of the bestselling book *Thinking, Fast and Slow*, is a psychologist whose research has looked into attentional effort: how concentrating uses up mental energy. He found that the less arousing or engaging something is, the more difficult it is to maintain concentration and the more effort we have to put in to stay focused.

Suppressing irrelevant input or distractions also takes mental energy, according to Kahneman. So, when you're trying to focus on, say, writing a book chapter, the more boring your subject matter, the more mental energy you'll have to exert, especially when your phone keeps buzzing, your dog is barking, and the targeted ads on your web browser are such good deals.[3]

It's true, though, that putting mental energy into something can be very rewarding. When a task requires our effort, whether mental, emotional, or physical, it tends to become much more valuable and meaningful to us than if we'd simply arrived at the outcome without spending any energy. This mental justification of effort is also called the *IKEA effect*: Laboring over a piece of furniture that we've constructed ourselves makes us value it much more than a piece we'd bought ready-made.[4]

Mental energy has also been linked with motivation. When we start a task, our motivation is usually high and we feel energized. As time goes on, we experience little wins and setbacks that make our motivation fluctuate. Sometimes our skill, combined with the desire for the end result, is enough to see us through, but on occasion a task will seem to drag on past the point of enjoyment so that we begin to reassess whether the energy cost is worth the predicted reward. When the cost seems too high and the reward too small, we experience low motivation, and fatigue will set in.[5]

But as engaging as this subject matter might be and as motivated as I am by my deadline and desire to hold the finished *Pace Yourself* in my hands, the process of coming up with sentences and witty remarks will eventually tire me out. If I try to push through the mental fatigue, I'll end up with poorly written paragraphs that have taken me three times as long to write as they would've done if I'd had a rest first or come back to writing in the morning after a night off.

I'll also use more energy if I'm trying to learn new information, though, like with physical exercise, the brainpower used for an activity gets less and less with practice.[6]

It seems obvious to say that learning uses energy or that concentrating takes mental effort; but we may not consider that some of our daily tasks that seem "low effort" are actually using mental energy. Back-to-back meetings, demanding high levels of concentration and equally high opportunities for distraction, can be exhausting. During the COVID-19 lockdowns, many teams moved their meetings online and learned that these can be just as tiring, leading to the coining of the phrase "Zoom fatigue."[7] Trawling through emails, coming up with new ideas, and even scheduling our days can all take effort, relying on our mental abilities to remember, assess, plan, and create. Yet we often underestimate the effect that these draws on our energy have on the rest of our lives.

On those days when we've spent hours at work focusing on something difficult or boring, we often don't give our minds a rest when we leave our workplace. We might drive home, which needs sensory attention (honking horns, flashing sirens) and the ability to engage quick reflexes (did you see that pedestrian step into the street?). If we stop off at the supermarket, even choosing between two similar items takes mental effort.[8] There in aisle ten, trying to decide between a bag of pasta and a slightly more expensive box of spaghetti, we automatically think of the choice in terms of the finances—depending on your current situation, you may consider that a) cheaper equals better for my wallet, or b) more expensive equals better quality. Whatever your mode of thinking, you might not notice that the box contains 50 percent more grams than the bag.

Using excessive amounts of both mental energy and emotional energy without respite can contribute to our levels of stress. When we subject ourselves to repeated stress, be that challenging tasks at work or a volatile relationship or even climate anxiety, our central nervous system puts us into fight-or-flight mode. Being in this high-alert state for lengthy periods has been shown to contribute to poor health: Our blood pressure rises, our arteries are more likely to clog up, and we can even cause changes within our brain that further impact our mood and anxiety.

There is no way to avoid spending mental energy, just as it's not possible to go through life without feeling a single emotion. Using our brain can be enjoyable and gratifying, and it doesn't have to take a lot of mental effort. Psychologist Mihaly Csikszentmihalyi identified the experience of effortless concentration in people so absorbed with a task, usually a creative one, and named it "flow."[9] The state of flow, or "being in the zone," isn't a place of low mental activity—depending on the person, you could be in flow while playing the piano, reading a book, even designing a website or manipulating images on Photoshop. These tasks still demand mental energy, such as remembering plotlines or assessing what looks good or bad, but when we're really absorbed in them, it feels like hours can go by without much strain.

Signs You've Exhausted Your Mental Energy

While the occasional long day at work is likely to make you tired, continuous mental strain can lead to exhaustion and problems not just in your job, but in the home, in your relationships, and with your health. Of course, we can't just structure our days around the activities that enable flow. We should, however, consider how we feel when completing mental activities, and ensure we have a good balance between expending energy and getting mental rest. A boom-and-bust pattern of mental activity feeds straight into our levels of fatigue: Too little exertion day-to-day can make us bored, affecting our mood and our motivation, but too much can lead to burnout, poor decision-making, and high levels of stress.

Using Too Much Mental Energy

It's still unclear why prolonged cognitive effort leads to fatigue, though different theories have been proposed and explored. One (now abandoned) idea is that exerting self-control directly used up stores of glucose,[10] while others have suggested the brain creates the feeling of fatigue when it perceives the cost of continuing a task to outweigh the benefit.[11] A promising new study, however, has found that continued mental effort actually leads to a buildup of a neurotransmitter called glutamate,[12] and proposes that this "waste product" of thinking could disrupt your brain functioning and make you feel fatigued.[13]

One of the most well-documented aspects of mental exhaustion is the **growing desire for easy choices and instant gratification**.[14] Think back on the decisions you've made recently—were they objectively sensible? Or have you been inclined to go for easy or instant solutions? You might also **be more impulsive**, maybe **spending money more often than usual** for a quick, small boost in mood.

Mental fatigue also affects your **ability to pay attention**.[15] You may find yourself easily distracted or **prone to procrastination**. Though procrastination can be a sign that you need to rest, as we'll discuss more in chapter 7, it's generally an indicator that you're unable to place your energy in a task. Sometimes you procrastinate because you don't feel you have the energy for a particular task, but instead of resting until you do feel up to it, you'll put your limited energy into something else. Or you procrastinate because you feel like the energy required by the task you *should* be doing outweighs the benefit. You may tell yourself things like, "Why should I spend all that energy crafting a CV when I won't get the job anyway?" or, "There's no point wasting all my time and energy on that assignment when I'll still just get an average grade." As mentioned above, when you're mentally exhausted, you're much more likely to take the easy route, and that includes opting for tasks that don't require lots of energy.

If the cause of your mental exhaustion is high levels of stress, then you're likely to have accompanying symptoms like **memory problems, anxiety, chronic inflammation, high blood pressure**, and **hormone imbalance**, to name just a few.[16] There is a Japanese word, *karoshi*, that means "death by overwork,"[17] and in most cases the medical cause of death has been a heart attack or a stroke thought to have been brought on by extreme stress.

Studies have also found a link between mental fatigue and **sleeping problems**. One study revealed people with a high cognitive workload have an increased risk of insomnia symptoms, including trouble falling asleep, waking up repeatedly during the night, and not being able to fall back to sleep once awake.[18]

In burnout, emotional and mental exhaustion combine to produce **feelings of cynicism**—about work, life, personal ability, and relationships.[19] This can range from indifference to active dislike and aversion to anything that requires your energy. Coupled with **low motivation** and procrastination, you can find yourself unable to complete even the simplest of tasks, but by no means are you resting. The guilt and negativity sap what remains of your energy, making it even more important to find ways to rest that don't drain you further.

Using Too Little Mental Energy

All the demands on your energy make it tempting to find low-effort solutions to problems. One principle that is referred to across psychology, biology, linguistics, and even in tech development, is the law of least effort. This asserts that things—human beings, animals, and even computers—will, when presented with a choice, choose the option that requires the least amount of energy.

In principle, it makes sense. It even seems aligned with the pacing lifestyle, in that your goal is to spend energy wisely, to make the most of life without burning out. Wouldn't the best way to do that be to spend as little energy on individual things as possible?

I think that while there are times when we should work to let things go rather than waste energy on being uselessly angry or anxious—to adhere to the law to "show no resistance" as Deepak Chopra writes—we should also be mindful of relying too heavily on the principle.[20] If it becomes your everyday solution to fatigue, you may find yourself taking mental shortcuts. You'll opt for quick, easy wins instead of pursuing longer-term, more difficult yet more rewarding goals. You might also be prone to procrastination, because busying yourself with small tasks seems more appealing than putting time and energy into that project you really should be working on.

While too much cognitive effort can cause fatigue, if you feel like you have no opportunity for challenge or development, you'll also find yourself lethargic and apathetic. Feeling stagnant at work or stuck with a problem can actually make you feel like you have less energy in general, because your brain wants to resolve the cognitive dissonance between the competing feelings.

Boredom can lead to feelings of fatigue.[21] When you're forced to use little mental energy, whether due to the repetitiveness of your job, an illness, or a lack of connection and engagement with the task at hand, you'll begin to have less energy to use.

Mental Exhaustion in ME/CFS and Long COVID

As with emotional activity, using your mental energy to the point of exhaustion can trigger post-exertional malaise, or PEM, in people with ME/CFS or long COVID. In my case, the symptoms of this type of PEM are mostly cognitive: brain fog, memory problems, and poor control over my attention.

For me, managing mental energy is harder than emotional or physical activity. My work demands a lot of mental effort, but use too much in one go and I'll pay the price in symptoms, due to the impact of PEM on my ability to do my job.

It's easy to forget that you might also use mental energy outside of a work context. Activities that are physical, like cooking or clean-ing, can also require cognitive effort.

Mental activity is a huge part of modern life. Children are taught the value of their minds from a young age, pitted against one another at school and then university. As such, the overall impact of mental energy can be disregarded and the warning signs of men-tal exhaustion are often missed. People with ME/CFS might notice that their friends, family members, and coworkers will struggle to understand why mental exertion can cause a flare in symptoms. To them, using your brain has always been seen as a good thing—how can it pose any real danger to your health?

This not only harms your relationships, but also their own health. If they can't appreciate mental exhaustion in you, they likely can't notice it in themselves. There's no easy remedy to a situation like this, but I try not to take their disbelief personally. If I have the energy, I'll try to educate them—maybe a copy of *Pace Yourself* would help?

Recharging Your Mental Energy

Though our brains literally never switch off, when your exhaustion is caused by too much mental exertion you can find rest through activities that put your mind into a kind of "low power" mode. This gives you the opportunity to restore mental energy and clear out any of the waste products of cognitive work, like glutamate.[22]

These activities will differ from person to person, and it will take a bit of experimentation for you to discover which work and which don't. As with emotional rest, the activities you use to recuperate shouldn't be thought of as unproductive or a waste of time. You know by now how detrimental exhaustion can be to your life.

It's hard to notice your own mental energy levels until it's too late, and in chapter 4 we'll discuss making feelings of energy more salient. But start now paying more attention to the things that demand your mental energy. Do you feel like you always have to be "switched on," reachable 24/7, and available to work at a moment's notice? Do you allow yourself to engage in activities that require low mental energy, or are you inclined to turn everything you do into another cognitive challenge? If you make all your hobbies into side hustles, only read books that are productive rather than reading for pleasure, and turn your commute from a fairly mindless trip into something intellectually stimulating by means of a podcast or audiobook . . . is it any wonder that you're exhausted?

There is nothing wrong with valuing mental effort, but it seems like this has been taken to the extreme for many of my generation. If you've learned to associate your self-worth with your mental output, you've probably extrapolated from this that any time spent *conserving* mental energy counts *against* your worth. In reality, you deserve rest and recuperation as much as you deserve respect for your achievements.

When you build mental rest into your day, you find that the hours you spend using mental energy are actually more productive and more enjoyable. You're less fatigued and so less distracted. You'll find that activity is less draining, so you might spend the same amount of time working but notice you feel better than before at the end of the day.

Activities that recharge your mental energy may use emotional or physical energy, and they may even need some cognitive effort, but they will likely be different than the mental tasks you do on a daily basis. If your job requires a lot of mental energy, it's important to find pockets of time throughout the day where you can get respite, even if it's only for a few minutes. I try to take regular breaks where

I give myself a low mental energy task, like making a cup of tea or watering my houseplants. During these activities, I make sure my phone is nowhere in sight, because I don't want to spend energy resisting the temptation to scroll on social media or check my emails.

> "When you build mental rest into your day, you find that the hours you spend using mental energy are actually more productive and more enjoyable."

When planning your own mental rest, start out by looking for activities that have one or more of these features:

- **Flow.** The feeling of being "in the zone" can alleviate some of the cognitive cost of activities. When was the last time you felt like nothing could distract you from the task at hand? It might be during physical exercise, or playing an instrument, being creative, or learning a new skill. Your mental rest might even be spending time with another person, eating at a new restaurant, or watching a film.
- **Mindfulness.** Similar to flow is the concept of mindfulness, which involves bringing your attention to the sensory experience around you and within your body,[23] while refraining from giving attention to thoughts and mental tasks that would take you out of the present moment. Mindfulness is a learned skill that can use mental energy, so it's not suited to everyone. I couldn't be mindful during meditation, for example, but I am able to experience mindfulness in situations that focus around one of my senses. The crashing of waves or the feeling of warm sand can aid in turning my attention away from imagination and into the present.
- **Mindlessness.** I first learned about mindlessness from neuroscientist Shane O'Mara, who describes it as "a kind of enjoyable mind-emptying."[24] For O'Mara, this state comes easiest

when out walking, without a deadline or particular destina-
tion, only the "freedom to just walk." Mindlessness seems
aligned with a period of low-arousal emotion, which can be a
form of emotional rest for those who spend much of their time
in high-energy emotional states.

- **Mindwandering.** Those who struggle with mindfulness might
  want to try its opposite, mindwandering. We often chastise
  ourselves and others when our attention wanders, but deliberate mindwandering—daydreaming, whether coming up with
  imagined scenarios or remembering past events—can alleviate some of your stress and actually put you in a more creative
  state of mind.[25] Letting your mind wander can lead some
  down the road of ruminating, to think anxious or depressed
  thoughts, however, so it may not be a suitable rest activity for
  everyone.

- **Play.** The mental pressures of work are easily shrugged off
  when you lean into activities of play and pleasure, which also
  often invoke a state of flow.

- **Exercise.** Haruki Murakami, whose novels have been trans-
  lated into fifty languages and sold millions of copies, takes a
  break from his writing with a physical form of rest: running.
  In his nonfiction book *What I Talk About When I Talk About
  Running*, Murakami explains that his writing practice is similar to his dedication to running.[26] He has to stick to his routine
  of writing in the morning, when his focus is at its peak, and
  then running once his work for the day is done. For him, running and writing are both long-term habits to build, and his
  commitment to one helps his dedication to the other.

- **Nap.** Some people find that a short nap during the day can
  help refresh mental energy, though it should be stressed that
  this highly depends on the individual—I find my fatigue worse
  after a nap, not better. According to science writer Dr. Stuart
  Farrimond, a four-minute nap boosts alertness slightly, while
  napping for ten to twenty minutes can improve your energy,

mood, learning, and productivity.[27] Don't doze for longer than half an hour, though, as you'll then be waking while in the deep sleep stage,[28] which will likely lead you to feel groggy and unrefreshed.

TASK

As you did in the last chapter, now come up with ten activities you could use as mental rest. Try to have a range of activities, paying close attention to how much time and energy they'll require—it's good to have some short, five- to ten-minute options as well as those that take an evening or last the whole day.

5 Principles of Pacing Mental Energy

1. Concentration, learning, and decision-making all use mental energy. As your energy depletes throughout the day, you may find each of these activities requires even more effort than usual.

2. Stress will exhaust both your emotional and mental energy finding ways to recharge that don't add to your stress levels will be really important here.

3. Conserving your mental energy can be a good thing, but using too little cognitive effort can make you feel bored, stagnant, or lethargic.

4. Don't allow your work or hobbies to have 24/7 access to your mental energy. The idea that you need to be "always on" or productive every waking moment has likely led you into your boom-and-bust lifestyle.

5. Some people find that mental rest activities allow their brains to switch off completely, while others prefer tasks that use mindwandering or enable a state of flow to recharge energy after a cognitively demanding day.

three

In Motion

Physical Energy

THE THIRD TYPE of energy to consider when pacing our lives is the energy we spend on physical activity. It's important to note right here at the start that "physical activity" is not the same as "exercise." In the scientific literature, physical activity is defined as "bodily movement produced by skeletal muscles that results in energy expenditure,"[1] though I want to make clear that activities that involve standing or sitting do still use physical energy, as keeping our posture requires certain skeletal muscles to contract or stiffen.

Exercise is thought of as a subcategory within the physical activity definition, the difference being that exercise refers only to activity that is "planned, structured, and repetitive" and has as its goal "the improvement or maintenance of physical fitness."[2] So, while vacuuming the floor is planned, structured, and repetitive, it's not likely to come under the umbrella of exercise unless your floors are already clean and you're just hoovering for the cardio. It is interesting that, even in people who exercise regularly, the majority of our physical energy is spent on non-exercise activities.[3]

As with the previous chapters on emotional and mental energy, I'll explain what physical energy is and what happens when we overuse it. Physical exhaustion, as I use the term, can refer to the fatigue felt when the demands on our physical energy far exceed our ability or when a lack of physical activity has directly contributed to low levels of energy. This particular fatigue is often felt as pain or lethargy in the body, but it'll also have emotional and mental symptoms, in the same way that emotional exhaustion and mental exhaustion both have some physical symptoms.

What Is Physical Energy?

When we think about the energy that powers our physical activity, we usually refer to the calories burned. A calorie isn't an ingredient like wheat or dairy, but rather a measure of the energy bound inside food, which is then used up, or burned, by our bodies. Every muscle movement requires calories, so scientists have been able to work out how much is needed to run a mile, or swim a length, or cycle up a steep incline. They've even calculated how much calorific energy is needed to sit at a desk and write a book, or to work as a firefighter or a hairdresser.[4]

While these figures tell us how many calories are needed for a task, they don't accurately represent how much energy we'll feel like we're using while we complete the activity. As you know by now, the perception of our own energy and fatigue is affected by many factors. Our motivation, our ability, our diet, and our sleep all impact our physical energy levels. Even our individual calorie use differs depending on things like our age, health, weight, and gender. Time of day can affect how many calories we're burning—after we eat, our body uses energy to digest our food, but one study found we burn 10 percent more calories in the early evening compared to the morning.[5]

As with mental energy, motivation plays a huge part in the physical energy needed for activities. In particular, a change or boost in our motivation when we're beginning to feel tired can renew our physical energy for a task, as evidenced by studies into endurance and sports science.[6]

Our physical energy is also tied to our mental and emotional energy. In nonathletes, mental fatigue has been shown to affect how quickly we tire when exercising, and the reverse is also true: Physical fatigue lowers our mental ability.[7] When it comes to our emotional state, just seeing images of happy or sad faces can change the feeling of effort while doing exercise; when smiling faces were shown to cyclists, they rode for longer and appeared to feel less fatigued compared to those shown sad faces.[8] And if you tell runners they look relaxed, they actually burn less calorific energy, even when running at the same speed as before.[9]

The amount of physical energy we need for an activity also depends on our ability. It seems obvious to say, but put me up against Usain Bolt and see who's more fatigued after a 100-meter sprint. But this applies to non-exercise activities, too. My husband, who worked as a chef for ten years, will need a lot less energy to cook a meal, whereas I'd find it way less taxing to write an article about said meal.

Over time, our ability to do physical activities improves, and the physical energy needed becomes less and less with each iteration. Our bodies are flexible and, if we treat them right, will work with us, not against us. This fills me with hope: Something that is too tiring for me currently isn't always going to be out of reach. If I pace myself, I can gradually work up to new physical activities, as you'll see is possible with any of your goals in chapter 10.

Of course, our ability to perform physical tasks like vacuuming or climbing stairs quickly reaches a plateau. There are only so many ways you can speed up household chores before you find the quickest, easiest way. Still, these activities benefit our overall health, with studies showing that low-intensity physical activity impacts our metabolic and cardiovascular health,[10] reduces risk of type 2 diabetes,[11] and enhances our immune system.[12]

"Motivation plays a huge part in the physical
energy needed for activities."

In our busy lives, it's tempting to cram all our physical activity into two or three sessions at the gym. You may do enough to meet the guidelines recommended by the UK National Health Service and the Physical Activity Guidelines for Americans: 150 minutes of "moderate" exercise or 75 minutes of "vigorous" activity each week. But reducing your physical activity to these short bursts may not be as beneficial as spreading your energy more evenly across the week. So, instead of having five fairly inactive days and two days of vigorous exercise, studies suggest that breaking up periods of sedentary rest with short amounts of physical activity can have a bigger impact on our overall health than infrequent blocks of hour-long exercise.[13] I'm not saying you should abandon your exercise routine, only that you should be wary of using your weekly workouts just to tick off "keep fit" from your to-do list. As you've learned in the previous chapters, physical activity can be a form of emotional and mental rest, and it's important to give yourself this restorative treatment in small doses as well as large injections.

Pacing your physical activity also spreads out the many benefits, which are evident at all intensities. Movement releases "feel-good" hormones like endorphins and dopamine, and though these are mostly produced during moderate or vigorous exercises, even simple movements can boost our mood. Getting our heart pumping faster sends more blood around the body, restoring oxygen and sugar to cells that are in need and potentially boosting our cognitive ability by flushing out glutamate, the waste product of some mental activity we talked about in chapter 2.

Physical activity can also improve our quality of sleep,[14] which leads to feelings of more energy—of all three types—the following day. Getting good sleep is crucial when you're assessing how much energy you have to spend, and we'll look more closely at your sleep in chapter 6.

Signs You've Exhausted Your Physical Energy

We have all experienced physical exhaustion in some form or another. But when this type of fatigue becomes persistent, it can be a sign that you're either using too much or too little physical energy in your daily life.

Using Too Much Physical Energy

When you use physical energy, especially for exercise, you are bound to feel tired afterward. Sometimes this fatigue lasts a day or two, and it might be accompanied by pain, tenderness, or a "local" fatigue in the muscles you've used. But this temporary exhaustion is usually resolved by physical rest and good-quality sleep. These two factors are key to reducing feelings of fatigue, because trying to push through and stay active, while having poor sleep, just exacerbates any feelings of exhaustion.[15]

If you continue to push yourself, however, **the effort needed for each activity only gets greater**, and each attempt to recover some energy gets less and less effective. **Your sleep quality declines,**[16] putting you into a vicious cycle—throughout the day your body will cry out for rest, but at night, you lie awake, unable to sleep, only to worry about all the things you will have to do on such little energy tomorrow. Your body is (barely) **functioning in a high-stress state**, which puts you at further risk of things like anxiety, depression, cardiovascular disease, and digestive problems.[17]

Regular exercise can strengthen your immune system,[18] but sleep problems and stress when you're physically exhausted make you **more susceptible to getting colds and infections.**[19] This puts further strain on your body, as an activated immune system has a high-energy cost.[20] Trying to push through viral or bacterial infection, such as with COVID-19, has been linked in some cases to the development of ME/CFS or long COVID,[21] though it's not clear whether this is a direct cause, or why those who do rest when ill can still develop the condition.

You may also notice **changes to your mood**. This might mean you feel things strongly, becoming more irritable or miserable. Or you may be more apathetic, unable to even muster the energy for negative emotion.

The lack of physical energy and lack of positive emotion can often lead to **relationship problems**. When you're exhausted, the last thing you'll want to do is socialize or dedicate time to romance, but as evidenced in the chapter on emotional energy, loneliness can be further exhausting.

Using Too Little Physical Energy

The "too much / too little" relationship between energy and fatigue applies to physical activity, too. Especially in those who've exercised in the past, too little physical activity in general will have a negative effect on our mood, motivation, diet, and sleep—all things you know link to your feelings of energy.

It's likely, then, that when you're physically exhausted, you'll find yourself opting for low-energy activity at every possible opportunity. But even though it may seem like you're resting, you're no doubt berating yourself for the inactivity. You might be worrying about all the housework you're putting off or be anxious about the impact your lack of communication is having on your relationships. If you're doing any of those things, you're using up emotional energy, and you have to question whether you're resting at all.

Adding more physical activity to your day, even if it's just ten minutes of cleaning or a walk around the office in between meetings, isn't naturally appealing, especially if you're exhausted. Your motivation to spend further energy across any of the three categories is bound to be low, and that just makes everything seem more effortful.

If your amount of emotional and mental energy is causing you physical symptoms of fatigue, it makes sense to address the imbalance in those activities before attempting to throw more physical demands into your already busy schedule. You do not have to change every aspect of your life at once to begin pacing. Once you've begun to feel less exhausted, you may find you want to start adding in small activities, but don't rush into anything. If increasing physical activity is one of your goals, you'll find the tools you need to pace yourself toward that goal in chapter 10.

Physical Exhaustion in ME/CFS and Long COVID

Studies of fatigue in people with certain health conditions, like lupus,[22] cancer,[23] and multiple sclerosis,[24] have found that exercise can reduce feelings of tiredness, but for people with ME/CFS, the introduction of more physical activity—exercise or otherwise—should only happen when you feel ready and want to increase your current level.[25] As mentioned earlier, pacing for people with my condition or long COVID isn't always about doing more, but doing what's possible within their current limits. I wanted to gradually increase my energy, so my pacing has always been designed in a way that encouraged experimentation with emotional, mental, and physical activity, pushing the limit little by little. But research into graded exercise programs for people with ME has shown that this can often exacerbate symptoms[26] as part of PEM and have a detrimental, long-term effect on overall physical and mental health.[27]

When I took part in graded exercise therapy a few years after being diagnosed with ME, my overall ability plummeted after each appointment with my physiotherapist. I was encouraged to do short exercises every day, even when PEM made my pain and fatigue flare up uncontrollably. After months of trying, I had to stop—my baseline health was worse than it'd been before, and I'd had to reduce activity in other areas of my life just to complete the painful few minutes of daily exercise. I resented my physiotherapist and what she'd told me to do, and that small slither of time set in stone my attitude toward exercise for the years that followed. I hated it. I was scared of it.

As I paced my way through university and into my first graduate job, my physical activity increased without my really noticing. I worked on building the amount of mental activity I could do each day, but it wasn't just my brain aiding my career: My body carried me through networking events and trips to research labs for interviews and photo shoots. So, when my coworker asked me if I'd like to join her bouldering one day after work—something I'd always wanted to try, thanks partly to that one scene in *The Princess Diaries*—I felt confident saying yes to exercise for the first time in nearly a decade.

Of the different types of energy, I now focus most on experimenting with my physical activity. There are so many things I want to do in life that involve physical energy—go wild swimming, try the world's fastest zip line, attend a roller disco—that I have made it a priority to include physical activities in my pace of life. But if you have ME/CFS and are happy with your level of physical activity or feel unable to increase it without jeopardizing other areas of your life, then please do not push yourself to your detriment. And, even if you do want to introduce more physical activity into your life, do not do so without the support of an ME/CFS specialist team.

Recharging Your Physical Energy

I always say that it is better to *choose* to rest than to be *forced* to rest. So, in this chapter, as in previous chapters, you're encouraged to come up with ways of incorporating physical rest into your pace of life.

As with emotional and mental rest, sometimes your chosen activities will still use energy, only it'll be in a form that isn't currently draining you. So, if your job involves standing on your feet for ten-hour shifts, you may choose restful activities that involve sitting down, but still use muscles in your arms. If you spend all day sitting, you may break up your work time by incorporating moments of standing, either at your desk or, better yet, outside in nature or in the company of others.

Other activities you could try as physical rest are:

- **Bathing and bodily self-care.** When your physical exhaustion restricts your activities, you can begin to view your body in a negative light. Reconnecting with your body through bathing or self-care activities, like massage and moisturizing, can alleviate some of this negativity. A hot bath, with or without added minerals and bubbles, has been shown to reduce the stress hormone cortisol.[28] Scientists aren't sure whether this effect is directly due to the bath itself or the opportunity to escape from busyness. If you can find a place for self-care—whether in the bathroom or a particular spot on your bed where you can't see things like your work computer or study notes—this will enhance the absorbing, relaxing nature of the activity. Reflexology[29] and massage[30] can also alleviate physical fatigue, so try taking a few moments at the end of a hard day to rub the parts of your body feeling particularly tired.
- **Hobbies.** As mentioned in the previous chapter, anything that puts you in a state of flow can act as rest and a distraction from fatigue. If your hobby has a physical element—pottery can be a strain on the body, and gardening is often labor-intensive!— try immersing yourself by watching others perform the activity on YouTube or TikTok.
- **Stories.** Reading, watching a film, or bingeing an entire series can offer physical rest. This is because being absorbed in a story can allow you to enter a flow state.[31] Even nonfiction and documentaries can be restful, you'll be glad to know.[32] If you find your mind wandering when you're watching or reading,

let it go: Daydreaming is rest, and you shouldn't feel guilty about indulging in it.

- **Sensory experiences.** Try restful activities that center around a particular sense. A hot bath an hour or two before bed, for example, helps you feel sleepy, which will be useful if your exhaustion is accompanied by trouble sleeping. If you don't have a bath, then using a bucket or bowl as a foot bath can have the same effects, as can heated socks.[33] You could try appealing to your sense of smell, using aromatherapy to reduce fatigue,[34] or listening to music or white noise.

- **Socializing.** Spending time with others isn't always restful, but physical fatigue can make you withdrawn and lonely. If you think that might be the case, try inviting a friend or two to join you for one of the restful activities listed above. Their company will be a distraction, but it can also enhance and prolong the desired effect.

- **Mental challenges.** Sometimes you might feel physically exhausted but bursting with mental energy. This can lead to feelings of guilt while resting, which make us more stressed and tired in the long run. If you can't shake off the feeling of needing to be productive (though I hope, by now, you've begun to feel more positive toward rest), you might find a mental challenge to be a suitable activity for physical rest. This could be crosswords, sudoku, puzzles, board games with friends, video games . . . anything that keeps your mind working and your body at rest.

* * *

While the signs of physical exhaustion tend to be more obvious, you can fall into the trap of only stopping to rest when you've pushed yourself so hard that you can't physically continue. You might even believe that your physical energy is inexhaustible, that if there are physical tasks that need doing—carpets to be vacuumed, washing to be hung out, exercises to be completed—then there is no time, and no reason, to stop and rest. In these cases, setting boundaries around your physical energy and communicating them to the people around you is even more important. When external (or internal) voices demand you keep going, you need to have the resolve to respond in favor of rest. Over time, seeing that your new pace of life is firmly set, these voices will quiet. The world won't end because you took a break.

> "It is better to choose to rest than to be forced to rest."

TASK

Write down ten activities you could use as physical rest. As before, include a range of activities, trying to vary their time demands, effort level, and financial cost. You'll use these, along with your emotional and mental rest activities, in chapter seven to build a Rest Bank that can be pulled from when designing your new pace of life.

5 Principles of Pacing Physical Energy

1. Physical energy is used in any activity that requires the movement of muscles. Exercise is a type of physical activity, but generally the majority of this type of energy is used in non-exercise activity.

2. The physical energy needed for an activity becomes less and less as you practice and improve your skills. This means that, though you may start off with very little physical energy available each day, pacing can help you to introduce more activity and start exercising in the future, if that is one of your goals.

3. Physical exhaustion impacts your sleep, your immune sys-
    tem, your mental and emotional energy levels. These effects
    make it even harder to regain energy, but physical rest can
    give your body a chance to recover and the opportunity for
    you to rebalance the amount of activity in your life.

4. In people with ME/CFS and long COVID, doing too much
    activity of any kind can exacerbate your symptoms. Exercise
    generally isn't recommended, especially in moderate-to-
    severe cases. If you do want to add more physical activity
    into your days, use chapter 10 to pace yourself gently toward
    this goal.

5. Experiment with different activities in your quest to recharge
    physical energy. The most important thing is to avoid feel-
    ing guilty about resting, which we'll talk more about in chap-
    ter 7.

four

Define

~~~~~~~~~

Your Current Pace of Life

NOW THAT YOU'RE FAMILIAR with the three different types
of energy, it's time to start identifying how they affect your current
life. The best way to do this is by keeping a pacing diary over the
next week or two, which we'll then use in chapter 8 to assess where
your energy is going and how you might be able to design a new
pace of life.

It's tempting at this stage to rush in and begin making big
changes in favor of saving energy. You might've already noticed
subtle ways in which learning about emotional, mental, and physical
energy has affected how you go about your days, or spotted a
boom-and-bust pattern in your life. But for the next week or two, I
strongly advise you to hold back on making any drastic alterations.

Consider the phrase "see the forest for the trees." This is what
we're trying to do with the pacing diary. We've already identified the
trees—the emotional activity being perhaps the weeping willow, the
mental activity as the grand oak, the giant sequoia as physical
activity—but we're still on the ground, under the canopy. Before we
begin felling trunks or planting seeds, we need to zoom out once
more and take in the whole forest.

The more information you can gather about your current pace
of life, the easier it'll be to spot patterns in your energy and

exhaustion. Why, then, am I only asking you to complete two weeks of the pacing diary? Why not a full month or more?

It's easy to get stuck at this stage. There's safety in observing, a false sense of progress while standing still. If you feel any reluctance about making changes to your pace of life, it's likely it'll present here as hesitancy to move on from the diary. Despite what you've learned about your own energy, you may still feel that your current pace of life is the only way to reach your goals. If that's true, then you'll naturally come to that conclusion at the end of this book anyway. But I expect you know that won't be the case. You know that your pace of living is unsustainable, but what you don't know yet is what your new life will look like, and that uncertainty is terrifying.

In the introduction we looked at teleoanticipation, the brain's tendency to set our future pace based on often misguided judgments about energy and success. The brain's ability to look into the future is one of its most important functions, and psychologist Daniel Gilbert has even called the brain an "anticipation machine."[1] Without our brain's ability to predict, we wouldn't be able to align goals with the actions needed to reach them. Yet this faculty relies on certainty. It uses past experience and knowledge about the future to make secure predictions.

Uncertainty stands in the way of the anticipatory brain. It shakes many of the foundations that hold up our beliefs about the world, and it's thought that chronic uncertainty could be a major factor in anxiety disorders.[2]

When faced with uncertainty, a natural reaction is avoidance. Avoidance behaviors, as psychologist Dr. Julia Ravey writes in *Braintenance: A Scientific Guide to Creating Healthy Habits and Reaching Your Goals*, are our brain's way of keeping us safe, reasoning that it's better to avoid a situation until we are sure of the outcome.[3] The best way to counteract this, says Ravey, is action. Facing the situation provides the brain with answers, so that bit by bit, as you move forward, you become less and less uncertain.

"The more information you can gather
about your current pace of life, the easier
it'll be to spot patterns in your energy
and exhaustion."

The Pacing Diary

When scientists are researching how depression affects a person's life or how a new drug might fit into the lifestyle of someone with an illness, they need to monitor their participants' daily activities. There are different ways to go about this, but for pacing, there are two you can use: real time or by reconstruction.

Completing a diary in real time requires a lot of effort from participants. They need to be able to make a note of whatever's needed throughout the day, and often for days or weeks without fail. Technology can be a massive help—a wearable blood glucose monitor makes it much easier for people in diabetes research to log their sugar levels at different points of the day and a smartphone app can help them record what they eat and drink with ease. Still, people can quickly tire of monitoring themselves all day, especially if it causes problems in other areas of their lives—I find taking a quick snap of a restaurant meal embarrassing enough, forget photographing my unattractive, bland sandwich that I eat at my desk for lunch or my coffee-stained mug during a work meeting.

The reconstruction method, on the other hand, is much less intrusive, though it's also less reliable. It involves writing a diary after the fact, relying on a person's memory to supply relevant information. This means you can go about your day without much distraction—no annoying ring of the alarm to interrupt whatever you're doing in order to document what you've just been engaged in and really ought to get back to. Kahneman and his colleagues used a reconstruction survey for their research on how people spend their time,[4] asking participants to reconstruct the previous day by writing a list of episodes or activities that had occurred during the day, noting where each event took place, who they were with, and how it made them feel.

My doctor recommended a real-time diary for pacing, and that's what I've used on and off for the last decade. I return to my pacing diary whenever life starts to feel out of balance, or when my illness relapses, as it can do in times of stress or poor health. Sometimes I only need to track my energy levels for a week or two to see where the imbalance is, but I have kept a pacing diary for months at a time when I've needed to.

TASK

I'd suggest that you start out keeping a real-time diary for at least the next two weeks. In chapter 8, we'll use your diary to uncover the areas where your own life is out of balance. The more data you have, the more confident we can be in the patterns it shows. But if you find that this method is too intrusive or intensive for your life, that's okay—a reconstruction diary will work, too. You can find examples of these in the Appendix as well as a printable template for both types of diary on my website, amyarthur.co.uk, but in case you'd like to design your own, here are the key aspects of real-time monitoring:

1. On waking, write down how much emotional, mental, and physical energy you feel you have. To do this, check in with each area, starting with the most obvious. If you've woken up from a dream, you might feel more in touch with your emotions coming out of that experience. Do you feel emotionally rested, ready for whatever comes your way, whether that's happiness or sadness? Does your body feel like it's had enough sleep, or have you been snoozing your alarm until the very last minute? Are you mentally energized, able to tackle the day's challenges, or burned out before you've even begun?

2. Throughout your day, note down every activity. Include the start and end time, as well as the types of energy you are using. Try to be specific. Instead of writing "work," "university," or "at home," break down your day into things like commuting, checking messages, attending meetings, chatting to friends and colleagues, making meals, and so on. The more detail you include, the easier it'll be to spot patterns in your energy expenditure later on.

3. Don't forget to write down any restful activities in your day. Include notes about the energy you are trying to recoup, and remember that activities that use one type of energy may provide rest from another.

4. Keep a note of what you eat and drink and how it affects your energy levels. Did your breakfast and cup of coffee give you a little boost of energy? Do you feel lethargic and slow after lunch? Is dinner hectic and draining, or pleasant and enjoyable?

5. Before you go to sleep, take a minute to reflect on the day's activity. How do you feel about where you spent your emotional, mental, and physical energy today? You might notice that you're more tired than usual, or even that you're too awake and still have some energy left.

• • •

If you're opting for a reconstruction pacing diary, you'll first want to find the right time of day for you to sit down and reflect. If you have five minutes in the morning, you can reconstruct the previous day, including all the activities you can remember and the types of energy they took to complete. If you get time to yourself in the evening, you might want to reflect on that same day, as it'll still be fresh in your mind. Whenever you manage to sit down, the key things to include in your pacing diary are the specific activities and how they affected your feelings of emotional, mental, and physical energy.

"The pacing diary sharpens our connection
with our own energy levels."

Noticing the Three Types of Energy in Your Daily Life

It's not always easy to identify feelings of energy. For a long time, you may have ignored signs from your body that you're running low on energy, so much so that you can't now distinguish between energy and fatigue in your day-to-day life.

In order for your energy levels to become salient, we need to make the feeling of energy noticeable and relevant.[5] You now know why energy is so important in life, so you likely feel it's much more relevant than before. To make energy noticeable, we have to use a little mental effort in the form of our attention. This is why your pacing diary is so important: The act of monitoring brings energy to the fore. Just as pedometers make us inclined to walk more and blood pressure cuffs help people manage hypertension, the pacing diary sharpens our connection with our own energy levels.

In an already busy life, I can appreciate the concern that completing a pacing diary could contribute to mental exhaustion. Here are some ways you can reduce the mental energy cost of noticing:

- **Use technology to your advantage.** I use an app called Toggl to keep track, in real time, of my time and energy. When I start an activity I'll open Toggl and write a little bit of information about the task—"writing" or "researching"—as well as labeling it with the type of energy it uses. Toggl will measure the time spent on the activity until I manually hit STOP, and start a new record for my next task. At the end of the day, I can see how many activities I've done and how much time I've spent on each, as well as the energy types used during the day. I give each type a color, so it's easy to tell when I've had an unbalanced day: A lot of red signifies an intense mental energy day, while a sea of green suggests I've used a lot of physical energy.

- **Make a habit of noticing.** The power of habit will be discussed fully in chapter 9 but for now it's important to know that forming a habit can reduce the amount of mental energy used for a particular task. So, if you're using the reconstruction diary to monitor your energy, try tying your note-taking to a preexisting habit. You could write your diary at the same time as having your first cup of coffee in the morning or after cleaning your teeth, but before getting into bed at night. By setting a rule for when you complete your diary, you're less likely to procrastinate or forget entirely.

- **Ask others for help.** If you feel comfortable talking about your energy with the people around you, see if they can identify instances when you're low or high on energy. Your colleagues might notice changes throughout the day that you're unaware of, or your roommates might comment on your fatigue on different days during the week. Having said this, other people are unlikely to have as keen a sense of your emotional and mental energy as you are yourself. Their observations may help you see how your fatigue presents externally, but it can sometimes be tough to hear how your struggles are affecting others. Energy is a sensitive issue, especially when you're exhausted. If you're feeling more vulnerable, consider whether feedback would help or hinder at this stage.

• • •

Part Two of this book can be read while you're still completing your pacing diary, so don't think you have to stop reading here for the next two weeks. The first chapter in the next part is all about your dietary choices and how they affect your energy levels, while chapter 6 will look at your sleep and includes some additional questions you might like to add to your pacing diary if you feel your sleep quality isn't as good as it could be. Chapter 7 will then consider your attitudes toward rest in more depth. At the end of Part Two, you'll identify your vital pace—the amount of activity you should be doing to stop your boom-and-bust lifestyle in its tracks.

5 Principles of Evaluating Your Current Pace of Life

1. Before you begin designing your new pace of life, you first need to understand the way you currently use energy and identify any boom-and-bust patterns. The way we do this is by keeping a pacing diary.

2. I recommend keeping your pacing diary for the next two weeks, but you can continue gathering information about your energy and activities for longer if you like. Be aware, though, that sometimes we can use the pacing diary as an excuse to stand still, to avoid making real changes to our pace of life.

3. I use a real-time diary to monitor my energy use throughout the day, as I find it much easier to jot down thoughts and feel-ings in the moment, rather than rely on my own memory.

4. However, you may find it easier to keep a reconstruction pac-ing diary. Picking a time each day to reflect on your activities and their impacts on your energy levels tends to require less effort overall.

5. The pacing diary should help make your feelings of energy salient. With practice, you'll be able to notice energy and fatigue in your body earlier, so that you can know when to rest and when to keep going.

part two
Assess

"Nobody realizes that some people expend tremendous energy merely to be normal."

—Albert Camus, *Notebooks, 1942–1951*

THERE ARE FEW THINGS within your control that have as big an impact on your energy levels as your diet and your sleep. The hours you spend asleep affect everything about your overall well-being, from your cognitive ability to the building and repair of your muscles, while your diet is the direct source of the energy that your cells need to support you day-to-day, to transmit information across synapses in your brain, and to send power to your limbs.

The next few chapters will focus on the things you can do daily to support your energy levels. Some of the advice given assumes you have some choice over the foods you eat, which may not apply to everyone and will be dependent on things like living situation, financial ability, and dietary requirements. Likewise, your sleep habits might be dictated by your work shifts, your kids' schedules, or your social life. Still, I hope there will be some small changes that you can try, whatever your individual circumstances.

This part is designed to be read while you complete your pacing diary. If you do decide to apply some of the recommendations for better sleep, diet, and rest to your own life, I would recommend you keep track of them in your diary.

five

Eating for Energy

SINCE YOU'RE RECORDING your daily food and drink intake in your pacing diary, this is a good point at which to look a little more closely at how your dietary choices are affecting your energy levels.

I'm sure you already know the basics of good nutrition: Eat fruits and vegetables, not too much sugar, stay hydrated, and so on. You'll also be familiar with the connection between certain foods and drinks and your feelings of energy. You might rely on caffeine to perk you up in the morning, or an energy drink after lunch to fight the early afternoon urge to sleep. I've always been partial to an eleven o'clock biscuit to "see me through until lunchtime."

When deciding what to eat, however, you're probably not thinking about what will be best for your energy levels. In particular, if you're low on mental energy due to a high-stress life, you're unlikely to be able to commit serious thought to planning meals and buying ingredients that can combat fatigue. My aim here, then, is to offer easy-to-follow advice that won't take too much of your energy to implement.

I can't offer you a cure-all diet, a meal plan guaranteed to wipe away all your feelings of fatigue. Instead, in this and the following chapter, you'll be encouraged to experiment with new habits and small changes that can help you have more energy in your days.

However, I caution against making too many changes at any one time, as this can easily become overwhelming and exhausting. Instead, opt for marginal gains that build over time and help establish long-term, sustainable change. Even an improvement as small as 1 percent can have a large impact, according to cycling coach Dave Brailsford. Before Brailsford, no professional British cyclist had won the Tour de France. Within three years, his 1 percent theory and belief in the aggregation of marginal gains gave Great Britain its first win.[1]

Small changes are more easily made and stuck with, and at the end of this chapter I'll ask you to choose a few ideas from those I've mentioned that you can apply to your own life. If you experiment with them for a couple of weeks and decide you'd like to add more, do so, but don't pile on too much at any one time.

Some of the advice in this chapter might seem counterintuitive or something you're sure won't work for you. Some of it, though, will involve changes that, deep down, you know you *should* make, but ones you don't really *want* to make. I really struggled to stop having my morning bowl of sugary breakfast cereal. I knew the science said it was likely causing a huge release in energy early on in my day, leading to a crash late in the morning and feelings of fatigue, but my sweet tooth always managed to sway my sensible brain.

In the end I told myself that I would try to go without sugary cereal for two weeks—just fourteen days—and I would see if my morning energy improved, or (more unlikely, I thought) if I found a breakfast I liked even better than cereal. This would be a "free trial" of the new habit before I decided whether to commit to a long-term subscription. After the two weeks, if I wanted, I could cancel with no regrets, moving on to the next new trial and shelving this one to revisit in future if I wanted.

Taking the pressure off new habits in this way makes them much more palatable, lessening the amount of willpower you need to start them in the first place, while freeing you from the guilt you might feel if you can't stick to them.

"Experiment with new habits and small changes
that can help you have more energy in your
days."

As you read through this chapter, keep in mind this free-trial approach and make a note of any changes you think you could implement for just two weeks. You may be surprised at how appealing something becomes when you think of it as only temporary.

Food as Fuel

Why do we eat? Food provides us with cellular energy, which is used by our muscles when we move, in the brain as it transfers information across synapses, and for a whole host of other functions that keep our body going. But we also eat to get essential nutrients, ones we can't make ourselves, and to replenish fat stores that keep us warm and act as an emergency reserve of energy. We also eat for pleasure—this isn't to be overlooked. When eating becomes habitual, boring, and uninspiring, we can find ourselves eating more than we need and feeling unmotivated and lacking the energy to make healthy changes to our diet and our lives.

There are plenty of great books out there that highlight the basic principles of a balanced diet, and I'll list a few of my favorites in the "Further Reading" section at the end of this book. However, there are some things I've learned about food, drink, and energy that I'll now share with you. Each "trial" suggestion is backed up by scientific research, but remember that what works for another person may not work for you in the same way. Use your pacing diary to keep track of changes to your levels of energy and fatigue so you can properly assess how your free trials have gone at the end of the two weeks.

1. Avoid Boom-and-Bust Blood Glucose Levels

The food you eat is broken down by your digestive system, with any carbohydrates or sugar in your meal getting turned into glucose molecules. These molecules are quickly circulated around your body to provide your cells with easy energy, while any excess glucose is to be stored away for later use. However, the speed at which your blood sugar rises and falls after a meal can affect your feelings of energy and fatigue.

If your meal is very sugary or full of carbohydrates and not much else, you'll see a resulting peak in blood sugar soon after eating. This is fine if you go straight into a workout where your muscle cells need a lot of fuel, but if the next thing you do after eating a bowl of sugared cereal is sit in your car or at your desk, you'll experience a blood-sugar boom followed by a fatiguing "bust."

This rise and fall in blood sugar levels is also referred to as glycemic variability[2] and it's extremely dangerous in someone with diabetes. But it can also have small impacts on levels of fatigue throughout the day in people without diabetes,[3] so it's worth trialing a diet that achieves a better balance of blood sugar.

This definitely doesn't mean you can't eat any sugar or carbs, but it does mean that you need to be mindful of the content of your meals and try not to have anything overly sugary if you're going to be needing consistent energy in the following hours. You should also try to pair carbohydrates with sources of fiber or protein, which can damp down the resulting blood glucose spike. Swapping your "refined" carbohydrates—plain potatoes, white bread, pasta, and white rice—for whole-grain versions is a great way to slow their release of energy.[4] If you can, opt for whole-wheat bread and pastas, brown, black, or wild rice, oats, barley, and quinoa. Or, if you want to use up your cupboard stores of white rice and pasta, try cooking and cooling them, as this has been found to increase the amount of fiber in each portion[5]—so cold pasta salads and sushi aren't off the menu! Potatoes don't tend to offer much in the way of fiber, but eating them with skins on will provide some, as will leaving them to cool in the fridge overnight.[6] To add more protein to a meal and slow the resulting release of glucose,[7] you could add meat, yogurt, or cottage cheese, eggs, pulses (beans, lentils, etc.), legumes, grains, or soy protein (tofu).

If you're going to test a diet that gives you more balanced blood sugar levels, I'd focus first on your breakfast. This is where most of us have high amounts of carbs (toast, cereal, etc.) with little added fiber or protein. What could you have for breakfast over the next two weeks that will lessen your boom-and-bust? If you're used to toast and jam, why not try whole-wheat bread with nut butter (just check that there's no added sugar in the spread)? I'm a big fan of porridge with a spoonful of peanut butter mixed in and chopped nuts and banana on top. If you have the time, you could trial savory breakfasts: Scrambled eggs and avocado or tomato sprinkled with some salt and chili flakes is often what I get out of bed for on a weekend!

2. Eat Balanced Portions

You know that a balanced plate of vegetables, carbohydrates, protein, and fat is important, but have you thought about your balance across every meal of the day? There is evidence to suggest that eating roughly the same amount of food at breakfast, lunch, and dinner is good for your health and for your mental energy levels, supporting your cognitive function into old age.[8]

Like many in the United Kingdom, your portion sizes might increase throughout the day, starting with a small breakfast, medium lunch, and large dinnertime meal. But consuming the majority of our food in the evening has been linked to an increased risk of type-2 diabetes,[9] metabolic syndrome, and nonalcoholic fatty liver disease.[10] It's worthwhile, then, mixing things up a little and experimenting with larger breakfasts and lunches.

If you're frequently skipping breakfast, you could be missing out on benefits to your cognitive function and mental energy levels.[11] If you usually grab a slice of toast on your way out the door, consider that eating more in the morning can decrease your feelings of hunger and any cravings for sweet treats and snacks throughout the day.[12] Feeling hungry midmorning really can make you "hangry," so you'll use more emotional energy being irritated or emotionally volatile.

The key word here is "larger" and not "massive." Too large a lunch will affect your afternoon physical and mental energy levels. Post-meal fatigue is caused by the release of sleep-inducing hormones, triggered when the gut is full. Your body wants to put all available energy toward digestion, so help lighten the load by avoiding foods you know are heavy in your stomach.

If you do find yourself feeling sleepy after eating, try going for a short post-lunch walk or spend just ten minutes out in the fresh air. Not only will it alleviate some of those digestion-associated feelings of fatigue, it's likely to aid your mental energy as we discussed in chapter 2. If the desire to sleep is too great, or if you're feeling particularly low on energy, you can try having a nap, but beware of sleeping too long during the day as it can negatively impact your ability to fall asleep later.

3. Eat for Brain Health

You know that if you don't eat well, your body will suffer. Your diet has the same effect on your brain. In particular, there are a few foods that can aid cognitive health and ensure you have enough mental energy throughout your day.

On every plate, the largest food group should be vegetables. Most experts recommend that 50 percent of the meal should be veggies, ideally with a proportion being leafy greens. These vegetables, which include things like cabbage, kale, spinach, and arugula, are especially good for our mental energy because they contain nutrients essential to our cognitive functions, like beta carotene, vitamin K, magnesium, and potassium.[13]

You don't really need me to sing all the praises of vegetables, but I can appreciate that introducing any new foods into your diet can be difficult, especially if you aren't familiar with how to cook them or are nervous about whether they'll taste good. There are a few things you can try to up your vegetable content:

- **Follow vegetarian and vegan food accounts on social media.** It's hard not to get excited to try some of the mouthwatering meals you see on social media. Somehow, Instagram chefs can even make salads look amazing. You might try setting yourself the challenge of cooking one new veggie recipe each week.
- **Dress up your greens however you have to.** Although dressings and sauces generally contain a lot of sugar and not much good stuff, I think they're immensely useful for getting you used to more vegetables in the first place. Once you're eating more, you can then try to wean yourself off them or make your own, healthier versions.
- **Grow your own.** Everything tastes better when it's homegrown. Lettuce, spinach, arugula, spring onions ... there are plenty of vegetables that will grow perfectly well on a windowsill or even at your desk in the office.

● ● ●

Your brain also needs you to eat fat because there are two types of fatty acid that are important for functioning but you cannot produce yourself. These are omega-3 and omega-6, and the only way for you to get them is through your diet, namely through oily fish and seafood, or nuts and seeds. For people who don't eat fish, you can take an omega-3 supplement, but if you can start a habit of eating a handful of nuts and seeds daily it will help with your good fat intake and aid your cognitive function and mental energy.[14]

4. Become Caffeine Conscious

If you rely on the energizing powers of caffeine, you might want to reconsider having a cup of coffee as soon as you wake up. This is because caffeine can disrupt that natural boost offered by your brain on awakening. If you can, wait an hour before drinking anything caffeinated to feel its effects without compromise.[15]

You might think your mental energy is improved with caffeine, but there is evidence to suggest that people who drink caffeine aren't any more productive or cognitively effective compared to those who don't.[16] Caffeine withdrawal can also make you feel more fatigued, so much so that drinking a few cups every morning can make you feel much more groggy and tired in the afternoon, having an overall negative effect on your energy levels. So, you could try going two weeks without drinking any caffeine and see if your mental energy levels are affected. You might replace it with a cold shower or at least a thirty-second jolt of cold water in the morning, which can boost feelings of physical energy.[17]

One general rule of thumb to stick to is to avoid ingesting anything caffeinated after 3:00 p.m., as it could remain in your system for up to ten hours, impacting your ability to fall asleep as well as the quality of your sleep overall. The lasting impact of caffeine varies greatly among individuals. You may have drunk cups of tea until bedtime for years with no problems, but it's worth putting a limit on your intake for a two-week trial to know for sure.

5. Hydrate

If you're feeling sluggish or slightly hungry, you might actually need a glass of water. One study found that even 1.3 percent dehydration, which most of us wouldn't even notice as thirst, can affect your mood, give you a headache, lower your concentration, and make cognitive tasks seem like they take more mental energy.[18] While hot drinks like tea and coffee, and cans of soda or glasses of juice, do provide us with water, they'll all affect your energy levels in other ways, too—through the caffeine or their effect on blood sugar. If you can, try to have some plain water as well as these drinks. Most people struggle to recognize thirst, so you'll want to have a glass or refillable bottle of water close by to remind you to drink regularly.

I struggle to drink enough water daily, but I've found that making the drink look *really* good is the best way to get my recommended six to eight glasses. That means adding either a few slices of lemon or cucumber, a sprig of mint, maybe a colorful straw, and, of course, some ice cubes, so that the beads of cold water run down the sides of the glass and add to the "drink me" effect.

6. Eat for Good Sleep

When it comes to your last meal of the day, it's good to make it a sleep-friendly one. Try not to eat too close to your bedtime, as it's not good to go to sleep while your stomach is busy digesting. For an evening meal that promotes good sleep, studies suggest eating foods that contain the amino acid tryptophan and the hormone melatonin.[19]

Tryptophan is commonly found in animal and plant protein, with the highest amounts in chicken, turkey, milk, bread, tuna, peanuts, oats, bananas, and dried prunes.[20] Melatonin is naturally produced in our brains throughout the day and it's thought that our internal body clock keeps track of rising levels of the hormone to determine when we ought to start feeling sleepy. Melatonin is sometimes prescribed by doctors, but it's also found in eggs, milk, grapes, cherries, tomatoes, mushrooms, pistachios, and other nuts.[21]

Some people find that avoiding fiber-rich foods in the evening helps, while others stay clear of acidic or spicy foods. Of course, there are plenty of people who regularly eat hot chilis or fibrous beans and legumes for their dinner. It comes down to your personal preference: If you want to try to get better sleep but enjoy your current diet, you might opt to make some of the changes in the next chapter before altering your evening meal.

7. Pay Attention, but Don't Obsess

Eating mindfully involves paying attention to each mouthful, chewing properly, and ideally not while distracted by your phone or the television. This helps your energy in a few ways: The more you chew, the less energy your body has to use for the digesting process; the more in tune you are with your sensory experience of eating, the more pleasure and positive emotional energy you'll feel; and you're more likely to notice when you're full if you're not distracted.

But, as with anything, you can take this and all of these suggestions to the extreme. Not wanting to be distracted while eating isn't a reason to stop going to restaurants with friends or having family over for dinner.

You can fall into a trap of overanalyzing your diet, stripping back each meal into its individual ingredients. There's even a suggested diagnosis for a person who has an unhealthy obsession with eating the "right" foods: orthorexia nervosa. But our relationship with food is more than the sum of its parts. Good food doesn't just provide our muscle cells with energy or our brains with nutrients. It can bring pleasure, pride, socialization, and stimulation.

Be wary, also, of under-eating. Undernutrition can lead to weight loss, while deficiencies in essential nutrients like vitamins and omega-3 can result in feelings of low physical energy.[22] If you don't get enough protein, fat, and carbohydrate in your diet, your body will begin breaking down fat and muscle cells to provide itself with energy.

This can easily become a vicious cycle, because when you're low on energy, you're understandably less able to shop for, prepare, and eat healthy, hearty meals.[23]

If you're concerned about your diet and its impacts on your health, it's worth consulting your doctor or a registered dietician before making any big changes. If you begin to feel ill at any point during your "free trial" of a new food or way of eating, stop your experiment and speak with your doctor.

> "Consider any new habits as 'free trials' that you can experiment with for a couple of weeks. If they make you feel better, you can take them on as permanent lifestyle changes."

TASK

Decide on one or two changes to your diet that you can try over the next two weeks. Continue writing your pacing diary while you complete these trials so that you can spot any changes to your levels of energy and fatigue and make an informed decision as to whether you'll be subscribing long term.

I encourage you to continue experimenting with your food and drink choices, trying new things whenever you feel able. A year from now, who knows how many will have stuck?

5 Principles of Eating for Energy

1. Making big changes can be daunting, so much so that we avoid doing the things we know are good for us in the long run. Consider any new habits as "free trials" that you can experiment with for a couple of weeks. If they make you feel better, you can take them on as permanent lifestyle changes, but if you decide they're not for you, that's okay, too.

2. Beware of a boom-and-bust pattern of energy levels caused by your glucose intake—try to balance carb- or sugar-heavy

meals with protein, or swap refined carbohydrates for whole-grain versions.

3. Upping your intake of vegetables can make a big difference to your mental energy levels and your overall health. If you find it difficult to think of ways to make eating veggies more appealing, find some vegetarian or vegan cooks to follow on social media for inspiration.

4. Eat with good sleep in mind. Try foods containing trypto-phan or melatonin in the evening and don't consume caf-feine too late in the day, ideally not after 3:00 p.m.

5. Don't obsess over your diet. Overthinking portion sizes or restricting your meals so much that you no longer enjoy eat-ing is only going to use more of your energy and reduce any benefits from the new habits you've tried.

six

Sleep in Focus

SLEEP IS AS IMPORTANT for good health and well-being as our diet, yet we don't put as much energy into designing a good sleep routine as we do in planning our meals. Your shelves aren't filled with sleep books, each detailing new ways to get better sleep, new combinations of pillows and blankets, or "detox your bedroom in five easy steps." You don't have to make a weekly list of all the things you need for good sleep or go around your house to check that you've got all the essentials: a cool room, no bright lights, a comfortable mattress, and so on.

When our body complains of dietary problems, we visit the doctor. But if you regularly sleep poorly, you likely try to "push through it." You might rely on caffeine or high-calorie meals to provide you with some energy. It's only when things get really bad that you might consider seeing your doctor, but your emotional, mental, and physical health will have suffered in the meantime.

In this chapter we'll look at the ways in which sleep impacts your levels of energy and fatigue. As with the previous chapter, there is a wealth of great books dedicated to the subject of sleep, and I'll recommend some of my favorites in "Further Reading" at the end of this book. However, these next few pages should provide some ideas for how you can improve the length and quality of your sleep.

Sleep deprivation can be extremely dangerous, but even having trouble sleeping for several nights every week can be a sign that something is amiss. You might think that insomnia is only when you go days on end without sleeping, but it's more common than that: If you struggle to get to sleep or to stay asleep for three nights every week for longer than three months, you may have chronic insomnia.[1]

Do speak to your doctor if you think your sleep isn't as good as it could be. It's worth adding a sleep section to your pacing diary before your appointment so that you're able to answer specific questions about your sleep habits. An example of this can be found in the Appendix.

How Sleep Restores Energy

Sleep is structured in stages, with each playing its own part in aiding your health and energy levels—not just for the following day, but over the course of your life. The four stages, which we'll go through now quickly, compose one sleep cycle. Your brain will complete this cycle several times during the night.[2]

The first stage of sleep is the lightest. It lasts for around ten minutes, before leading to the second stage. Slightly deeper, in the second stage of sleep your body and mind begin preparations for the third state, like the last person leaving the office going around and closing the blinds, turning off the lights. The third stage is what's called deep sleep, or slow wave sleep.[3] Deep sleep is considered the "most refreshing" stage.[4] It's thought that in deep sleep, the focus is on bodily energy restoration, while the brain is in a stage of low energy, or conservation.[5] Deep sleep also repairs muscles and stimulates growth of new tissues and cells,[6] all of which contribute to better energy storage and supply to your body during the day.

Lack of deep sleep has been linked with anxiety and stress, with one study finding that a single sleepless night can cause anxiety levels to rise by 30 percent.[7] This will, of course, have an impact on your emotional energy for the following day, making you tend toward negative, high-arousal emotions.

After deep sleep comes rapid eye movement sleep, or REM sleep. This is the only stage in which you dream, thought to be because REM sleep is when your brain is most active—consolidating memories, processing things you've learned during the day, and checking that all cognitive functioning is in good, working order.[8] REM sleep is also key to maintaining levels of emotional energy in the day. A lack of REM sleep has been found to cause emotional instability, causing a person to swing from overly positive to extremely negative emotional states. This can easily lead to emotional exhaustion. Dr. Matthew Walker, scientist and author of the book *Why We Sleep*, argues that the advancement of emotional processing is the most influential function of REM sleep.[9] This sleep stage is also important for creativity, as the sleeping brain is free to explore ideas and connect seemingly unrelated thoughts and memories in ways your waking self would never attempt, to result in "some of the greatest feats of transformative thinking in the history of the human race," according to Walker.

Sleep not only restores energy: It also ensures energy is not wasted. A day spent using mental or physical energy to learn—whether that's developing a new skill, improving an existing ability, or acquiring knowledge—needs to be followed by a good amount of sleep in order to truly stick. After a good night, performing your new skill or recalling your learning will come more easily and therefore use less energy.[10] On days where you've used a lot of physical energy, sleep helps your body to reduce the slight inflammation caused by activity, while also stimulating your muscles to be repaired and your cellular stores of energy to be replenished.

Chronotypes and Your Energy Levels

Things that contribute to your feelings of energy, like alertness, motivation, and stress, fluctuate throughout the day. These fluctuations are linked with your chronotype, which is the preference of your internal body clock for activity.[11] Chronotypes are thought to be on a spectrum that ranges from morning types (or "early birds") to evening types ("night owls"). About 21 percent of adults are night owls while 14 percent are early birds; the rest of us fall somewhere between the two.[12] Morning types are found to have peak energy levels around late morning to midday, while evening types feel a gradual increase in energy over the day, peaking in the evening.[13] However, this particular study wasn't looking into a specific type of energy, just general energetic feelings held by individuals.

There is a questionnaire that you can take to find out your chronotype, which you can find in the Appendix, although you may already have an idea of whether you're more of a morning or evening person. It's likely that your preference will change over your lifetime, and it's certainly not the only determining factor for your energy throughout the day. A good diet and prioritizing quality sleep are still going to have a big impact on your levels of emotional, mental, and physical energy each day.

What Is Good Sleep?

Generally, seven to eight hours of sleep each night is recommended, though some people need slightly more or slightly less to function at their best. Less than six hours of sleep every night, however, will be harming your energy levels, and you'll find yourself getting exhausted more quickly.[14] You'll also affect the ability of your heart to pump blood around your body, the amount of oxygen your lungs take in, how easily your cells can access energy, and even things like your internal temperature regulation.

If you think your sleep could be improved, you're not alone—nearly a third of people around the world are thought to have trouble sleeping.[15] There are many things that could be causing your problems, not all of them negative. Yes, stress and poor mental health will impact your sleep, but sometimes we give away our shut-eye willingly, choosing to stay out all night or work to a deadline until the early hours. You might've made a big life change recently and seen an impact on your sleep: A new job, sharing a bed with someone new, and becoming a parent will all upend your usual routine.

The amount of sleep you need changes as you age, with teenagers wanting two full hours more each night than older people. Health conditions, menstrual cycles, perimenopause, and menopause can all affect sleep quality.

However, if you find you're in a boom-and-bust pattern of sleep, spending a long time in bed some nights and barely letting your head touch the pillow on others, you might want to try some of the suggestions in this chapter. In particular, if you regularly sleep less than seven hours, or nine or more, you may want to try a "free trial" period of seven or eight hours of sleep. Stick to this as rigidly as you can for two weeks to see if it has any impact, positive or negative, on your levels of energy and fatigue. Of course, if you notice any really detrimental effects on your daily living, don't continue your trial for the sake of it—listen to your body if it tells you something isn't right.

Signs of poor sleep include:

- Taking longer than thirty minutes each night to fall asleep from the time you go to bed
- Making excessive snoring or choking noises during the night, usually noticed by a bed partner (this can be a sign of some sleep disorders, so it's worth mentioning to a doctor if it occurs regularly; in other words, three or more nights every week)
- Waking up feeling unrefreshed or like you haven't had enough sleep despite being asleep for eight hours or more
- Having to rely on caffeine to function normally

• • •

Pacing can help with some of the causes of sleep problems, like stress and a boom-and-bust sleeping pattern, but it's important to identify and accept anything that can't be changed about your situation. Sometimes, our sleep, as with our energy, is at the mercy of circumstance. If you're living with a young child, there's probably not much hope of getting a full seven hours every night of the week. If you have ME/CFS, you may feel the need to sleep much longer—when my own condition was more severe, I would sleep between ten to twelve hours each night—but it's likely that your sleep quality is poor and you wake up feeling unrefreshed no matter how long you've slept.[16]

There will be "small wins" to be had, though. Anything you can do to squeeze in a few more minutes of shut-eye is worth it, as are any changes that can improve the quality of sleep you *do* get. Don't feel you have to tackle everything at once: Focus on one issue with your sleep at a time to avoid overwhelming yourself, which will just cause more stress and make good sleep more elusive.

Difficulty Falling Asleep

Ideally, you should fall asleep in less than thirty minutes from the time you get into bed. Any longer and it's likely you'll start worrying about your need to get to sleep, which only raises your stress levels and makes sleep even more elusive. Or, you'll begin to ruminate over the day's anxieties or tomorrow's to-do list, again, increasing your alertness and making it less likely you'll drift off.

If this is a common occurrence for you, try the following:

- **Perfect your sleeping environment.** Block out as much evening light as possible to aid sleep. If you've got the technology, you could even try simulating sunset in your room, dimming the light gradually in the hour before you intend to sleep. A room temperature of between 15°C and 20°C (60°F and 68°F) is thought to be best for sleeping, though again this depends on personal preference. Experiment with your environment to find out what works best for you.

- **Teach your brain when and where to sleep.** Having a night-time routine really helps your brain prepare for sleep. A regular drink before bed, or a certain scent, can create an association between the habit and sleep and put your brain into "shut-down" mode. You should also have strict rules about where you sleep. Ideally, your bedroom should be for sleep only—keep work and play outside the door (although scientists and doctors agree that sex is permitted!). If you have to use your room for other functions, separate your space as much as possible and keep your bed off limits.

- **Save your technology for daytime only.** Screen use close to bedtime has been shown to affect sleep quality.[17] Whether this is completely due to the blue light emitted by screens is debated, as it could be that the stimulation of your brain makes you too switched on for sleep and leads to less REM sleep when you do nod off. If you can, try to have thirty minutes of no screens—that's no phone, TV, or video games—before you lay your head on the pillow. It's a tough free trial to take on, but you might be surprised at how much of an impact it'll make. Instead, you could read a book, work on a creative hobby, indulge in a new self-care routine, or go for a light walk.

- **Don't allow ruminations to spoil your sleep.** If you're struggling to sleep and have been wide awake for thirty minutes or more going over all your worries or your endless to-do list, the best thing you can do is get out of bed. Honest. I know it's hard to get up, especially if you're cozy, so make the task as appealing as possible. Pull on something warm, treat yourself to a glass of warm milk, hot chocolate, or chamomile tea, and sit somewhere where you can't see your bed. Read, write down your anxieties, meditate, or daydream until you feel sleepy.

- **Avoid exercising too close to bedtime.** Evening types might feel they have a lot more physical energy after work, in which case they're likely to prefer exercising before or after dinner.

Exercise will increase body temperature and cause the release of the hormone cortisol, which heightens alertness and gives a little boost in mental energy. Both these effects are likely to delay sleep onset, so try not to do intense physical activity in the hour or so before bedtime.

Problems during Sleep

When you wake up in the morning, do you feel unrefreshed despite having slept for seven or eight hours? Or do you find yourself waking up often in the night, unable to stay asleep for any length of time?

Given how important deep sleep and REM sleep are for your emotional, mental, and physical energy, it would be useful to check that you're getting enough time in these stages. However, that's not easily done outside of lab conditions. While sleep trackers and fitness watches can monitor your heart rate to differentiate between activity and rest, those currently on the market aren't necessarily reliable indicators of time asleep or at picking out different sleep stages.[18]

Instead, focus on the factors within your control. This means:

- **Being aware of how alcohol affects sleep.** Alcohol before bed can reduce the amount of REM sleep you get[19] and for some will lead to more awakenings during the night. If you're prone to sleep talking or sleepwalking, you'll find instances more common after evening drinks.
- **Addressing snoring.** If you snore, you're likely disturbing your own sleep without realizing it. This can make you feel unrefreshed even if you've been in bed for the recommended time. You might feel a little uncomfortable going to the doctor to discuss snoring, but if it's really affecting your energy levels, it's worth investigating. Treatment can be simple, but what works will depend on what's causing your snoring, which your doctor should be able to identify.

- **Treating insomnia.** If you have several bad nights every week, you may be suffering from insomnia. If you have insomnia, when you do fall asleep you'll likely have poorer-quality deep sleep and REM sleep, and wake up feeling tired.

Trouble staying asleep and unrefreshing sleep can be linked to a number of sleep disorders, such as sleepwalking and sleep apnea, but it's also a symptom of conditions including ME/CFS, fibromyalgia, depression, and even chronic stress.

Poor sleep can make you want to nap during the day, but it's generally not recommended, as napping can confuse your internal body clock and likely make your overall sleep quality decrease.[20] The exception here is when your lifestyle means you can't ever get enough hours in the night—parents and shift workers often have to take whatever sleep they can. Ideally, these situations are tempo rary. Sleep deprivation for any length of time can do damage, but after a few years it becomes more important than ever to prioritize a good sleep routine.

Most sleep scientists agree that you're also unable to "catch up" on lost sleep during the week by sleeping in on the weekend. According to one study, a single hour of sleep debt takes four days of good sleep to recover.[21] Sleeping in can be lovely, but don't rely on that as a way of getting around your sleeping needs during the week.

Trouble the Morning After

When your brain transitions between sleeping and waking, it naturally experiences a state known as sleep inertia. Your mental energy, though refreshed in the night, isn't immediately accessible—you wouldn't perform brilliantly on a math test if someone started questioning you in this period. Your body doesn't respond to instruction as quickly as usual, and you might feel a desire to go back to sleep. Though typically brief, sleep inertia can last a couple of minutes to several hours.[22]

It's thought that sleep inertia evolved to protect the sleeping brain from unwanted awakening.[23] You can imagine your ancestors benefited from sleeping through small noises and movements, as it would be tricky to get a restful night if every rustle of leaves in the breeze jolted them awake. Sleep inertia isn't so powerful that it can't be overcome in times of need, however: Your desire to sleep wouldn't win out against your instinct to leap out of bed if someone shouted "fire!" for example.

While sleep inertia is a result of waking up naturally, most of us don't rely on our own bodies to wake up on time. Nor do we always get up as soon as the alarm rings. But how often you snooze your alarm can impact your feelings of energy at the start of the day.

An alarm jolts you awake, bypassing sleep inertia and stimulating the release of several hormones in our brain to quickly take us from sleep to consciousness in what's been a "stressful awakening."[24] Repeatedly snoozing your alarm on a morning may be making you feel like you have less energy because it leads to several of these sudden and stressful awakenings in a relatively short amount of time, leaving you mentally tired. It can also contribute to a low morning mood and lower emotional energy during the day. Years of these stressful awakenings will also contribute to the clogging of your blood vessels and increase your risk of heart problems later down the line.

From the moment you wake up, your brain works to get from sleep inertia to full consciousness. A slew of hormones and neurotransmitters are released that encourage alertness and reduce the desire to sleep. This only happens if you keep your eyes open, though. If you manage to nod off and find you've inadvertently added an hour or more to your total sleep time, you're likely to feel less motivated and energetic when you do stumble out of bed. Sleeping in leads to lower mental energy in the morning because you've missed that natural boost in energy your brain provides, and you'll feel comparatively more groggy and tired.[25]

This means that finding and sticking to a sleep routine is key to starting the day with good energy levels. If you can, choose a gentle alarm and don't hit SNOOZE. This is a really good "free trial" to start off with, as it can make a significant difference to your morning. Try it for two weeks and be sure to reward yourself if you manage it—breaking a habit you've likely had for your whole adult life is no easy task.

"Finding and sticking to a sleep routine is key
to starting the day with good energy levels."

A Note on Shift Work and All-Nighters

It's well known that shift work is bad for your health, in more ways than one. When you work nights, your sleep–wake pattern is at odds with your internal body clock. This is explained in much more detail by Professor Russell Foster in his book *Life Time*, as well as in Walker's *Why We Sleep*.

But what about the odd all-nighter? If you're a student or have a job that sometimes involves late evenings and early mornings, like law or care work, you've likely given up sleep so that you can work.

You might be surprised to learn that just one night of sleep deprivation has been shown to affect our cognitive performance[26] and our ability to recognize and regulate emotions.[27] In a study of university students, those who deprived themselves of sleep to study for an exam were found to have reduced their brain's ability to retain what they learned by up to 40 percent, compared to students who'd gotten a full night's sleep.[28] I don't know if any of those students were parents, but I'm willing to guess that anyone looking after young children is well aware of the impact of broken sleep and lost time.

The trouble is, while you *can* skip breakfast, live off microwave meals, or rely on protein shakes during tough times, there is no real replacement for sleep.

Whatever the reason for your lack of sleep, it's important to make concessions to allow for the impact on your health, energy levels, and emotional state. If you know in advance that you'll be dealing with less sleep for a while—maybe next month you're traveling to a vastly different time zone, expecting a baby, or scheduled for surgery—plan to reduce other activity as much as possible. On less sleep, you won't have as much emotional, mental, or physical energy, and normal tasks may take more effort and time than usual. Make sure the people around you are also aware so that they can manage their own expectations of you. Go easy on others, too, knowing that your ability to regulate emotions or tolerate stress is reduced when you're tired.

In the long term, prioritize good-quality sleep wherever possible: It really is crucial for your emotional, mental, and physical energy. One lousy night is bound to happen every now and then. If you find you've not slept well, go easy on yourself and try to reschedule high-energy activities for another time—don't push yourself to meet a schedule set by a well-slept version of you. If you find you're regularly having problems sleeping, though, it's worth speaking to a doctor to see if something is amiss.

TASK

Pick out one or two ways you could try improving your sleep. As with the previous chapter, it would be useful for you to continue writing your pacing diary while you try out your new sleep habits so that you can assess the impact to your levels of energy and fatigue.

5 Principles of Getting Good Sleep

1. Sleep is how your body restores the energy you use during the day. In particular, deep sleep helps your body store and supply energy more efficiently, while REM sleep helps

emotional stability and ensures any energy used has not been wasted by consolidating memory and learning.

2. Your internal body clock will have a natural preference on a spectrum of chronotypes. You might be more of a morning person, favoring peak energy use around late morning or midday, or you may lean toward an evening chronotype, whereby you're alert and motivated later in the day. Understanding your body clock is useful for setting routines, but it isn't the only factor to consider when designing a good sleep schedule.

3. Ideally, you should be getting between seven and eight hours of sleep each night, but there are many reasons why your actual time in bed might be more or less than this. If you can, try to avoid a boom-and-bust pattern, where you're sleeping a long time one night followed by very little sleep the next few nights. Stability will do you more good, as "catching up" on lost sleep is difficult to achieve.

4. If you do have a bad night, make allowances for yourself and others the following day. You'll likely have less energy, find it hard to concentrate, and struggle to control your emotions. Do what you can to limit the energy demands of activity and reduce your expectations—you don't have to perform the role of a well-slept version of yourself.

5. Remember to work on a "free trial" basis, only selecting a few changes to make at any one time. The more pressure you put on yourself to solve all of your sleeping problems in one go, the more energy you'll end up using.

seven

Rest to Recharge

~~~~~~~~~~~~~~~~~~~~~~~~~~~~~~~~~~~

WITHOUT ENERGY, there would be no life on Earth. A long time ago—3.8 billion years, according to NASA[1]—the first organisms somehow managed to take in energy from the molecules around them. Since then, energy has been the currency of life, with each living organism finding a way to obtain and use its own source.

Those who evolved better ways to use and conserve energy became much more likely to survive. The warm-blooded animals that lived in colder climates would lose a lot of energy as heat if they didn't grow warm, thick fur. Plants on the rainforest floor that were shaded by the tall trees towering over them benefited from growing larger, greener leaves that could absorb more sunlight to turn into energy. Early humans who encountered a predator would run from danger of death—the ultimate loss of energy—benefiting overall from the cost of powering their legs.

"Survival of the fittest" was really "survival of the most energy-savvy," then. Conservation and better management of energy was paramount to continued life on this planet. That could be why we respond so favorably to high-calorie foods: In the past, anything that gave us more energy was an advantage.

But natural selection by evolution wasn't a conscious process. The bear didn't decide to grow more fur to keep himself warm. It was just that the environment he found himself in was more tolerant of certain traits and less obliging to others. If his offspring had less fur, it'd have less chance of survival and less opportunity to pass along the unfortunate variation.

This unconscious preference for certain characteristics above others once taught us to conserve energy. Today, the environment around us is such that we reject any notion of resting. Life now dictates that energy is to be used, always, because that is how to survive. The more you do, the better you live.

Perhaps you feel as if each day's energy is used only to keep up a pace of life that you didn't set yourself. Maybe the majority of your energy is put toward making enough money to meet your basic needs, while what little is left has to be spread across everything else that your life demands, be it socializing, cleaning, exercising, or taking care of family. Perhaps you're pursuing a degree that you never really chose, feeling funneled down a path based on your best grades in school. Your day may be entirely dictated by the energy needs of another: When you're running around after children, trying to keep them well fed and entertained and out of harm's way, rest seems like a laughable luxury.

Even the "energy-saving" devices that you have access to contribute to the overall feeling that reserving energy is bad. Instead of walking, you can drive; forget cooking, use a microwave; why make coffee when you can get it on the go? These things were built to make life easier, but how do you use that energy saved? Realistically, their impact is barely noticeable. Any conserved energy is just put toward doing *more*, because we've become a society that sees more as *better*.

Idle Hands Are the Devil's Workshop

The truth is nobody likes to be idle. We dread boredom and tire of waiting, while busyness and achievement are revered. But why? Where has this idleness aversion come from?

Somehow, we have become convinced that to stop pursuing things—goals, accolades, money—is to be lazy. That all the things we have achieved thus far and the successes still to come are in jeopardy the moment we stop striving for them. That, if we stop working, even for an hour, someone could come along and take away our opportunity to ever work again.

Many people hold meritocratic beliefs, that rewards and advancement should be allocated to those who earn it, who put in the effort and perform above and beyond. Even understanding that our achievements are also influenced by our genetics, the culture and class we were born into, don't we all want to be valued for what we do?

Equating reward with effort comes at a cost. Reward is seemingly infinite: There is always more money to be made, higher positions to hold, and awards to be won. There is no final end point, to refer back to the teleoanticipatory brain we discussed in the introduction.

In striving for something infinite, we assume our effort also has to be limitless. We hold ourselves and others to unreasonably high standards, demanding time and energy above and beyond what we have to offer. It's no surprise that this is one of the conditions in which burnout occurs.[2]

This has led to the notion that busyness and a lack of leisure time is a sign of high social status.[3] When people say, "I'm just so busy!" we instantly assume this is a reflection of how competent they are, how in demand. To say, "I'm not very busy," would be to say, "I'm not putting in enough effort," or "I'm undeserving of reward."

In fact, psychologists Adelle Yang and Christopher Hsee argue that people are so averse to idleness that they pick and pursue goals just to engage in activity.[4] Doing *something* is always seen as better than doing *nothing*.

It's strange, though, that the phrase "idle hands are the devil's workshop" is so common, considering the importance of a day of rest in many religions. According to writer Judith Shulevitz, the

Israelite Sabbath set out that everyone should observe the day of rest, women and slaves included—that's how important the practice was.[5] As time went on, religious beliefs influenced secular policies, as Sunday trading rules and "blue laws" were set to limit work and activity one day a week.

Now, we don't even want to rest for a few hours after work, let alone a full day. When we do rest, we berate our character and lack of dedication. What will it take to allow ourselves to rest?

Allowing Yourself to Rest

Rest in pacing is time that allows you to replenish your energy. You know that using too much emotional, mental, or physical energy can lead to exhaustion, but that there are activities to restore each of these types of energy. Rest is just as important for your mind and your emotions as it is for your body.

In physics, an object at rest has zero velocity; it has no speed or movement. To satisfy the physicist's definition, your lungs would stop breathing, your heart stop pumping, your brain stop sending messages across synapses. You can, by that logic, only rest when you're dead.

It is interesting that the physicist's concept also allows for an object at rest to have forces acting upon it, but those forces must balance out so that there is no motion. I think, then, to truly rest, you must be able to acknowledge any pressure being applied by the ideas of "busyness is good" and "idleness is weakness," while applying your own firm insistence that rest is what you need and deserve.

If productivity is all that matters to you, then the negative impacts of exhaustion on your attention, memory, and performance should reassure you of the worthiness of rest. But you are not a machine, defined only by your output. You are a living being, a thing that has always made compromises between activity and rest, understanding that conservation of energy is as key to survival as gaining energy through diet and sleep.

Just as you make time throughout the day to eat, you should make time for rest. There will, of course, be times when you opt for a sandwich on the go, or skip breakfast to make your train. Sometimes, external factors dictate when and how you take your mealtimes. In the same way, you might not have control over your working hours, the commute, your kids' activities, and your social appointments. You can, however, make the commitment to prioritize small moments of rest over unnecessary additions to your already bursting schedule.

"Rest is just as important for your mind and your emotions as it is for your body . . . What will it take to allow ourselves to rest?"

What Is Rest?

In the Rest Test, a study of more than 18,000 people from 134 different countries, it was found that those who felt most rested also had the highest scores for overall well-being.[6] These were people who had between five and six hours of total rest across the day. How does that compare to the activities in your pacing diary? It sounds like a lot of time but remember that rest doesn't mean inactivity. The below list shows the twenty most popular restful activities from the participants in the Rest Test:

1. Reading
2. Looking at, or being in, a natural environment
3. Spending time on your own
4. Listening to music
5. Doing nothing in particular
6. Walking
7. Taking a bath or a shower
8. Daydreaming

9.   Watching TV
10. Meditating or practicing mindfulness
11. Spending time with animals
12. Spending time with friends/family
13. Making/drinking tea or coffee
14. Engaging in creative arts
15. Gardening
16. Traveling on long train journeys
17. Engaging in physical activity
18. Chatting
19. Drinking socially
20. Eating

• • •

Now consider how much time you spend undertaking any of the above activities throughout the day. How close are you to matching the five to six hours of the most well-rested? I'm not suggesting that this is the optimal time of rest, especially because there are many people with ME/CFS and long COVID who need much more. At my worst, I could only manage an hour and a half of activity each day, leaving me with a good fourteen and a half hours to fill. Just like the Rest Test participants who had more than six hours of leisure time each day, I found the experience more frustrating than calming.

Yet finding the right restful activities is just as important as getting a good amount of rest. It is interesting that many of the activities listed are solitary pursuits. People prefer to rest alone. The first mention of being in another's company is at number 11, and actually, that activity is spending time with animals, which was slightly preferable to being with friends or family at number 12.

Of course, some will use vacations as times of rest. You may spend a week by the pool, lounging, reading a book, going for a swim, and daydreaming (items 5, 1, 17, and 8 of the Rest Test list).

But be wary of relying too heavily on the impact of a week's rest compared to fifty-one weeks of stress and exhaustion. Not to mention that vacations, too, can be stressful and exhausting.

In Part One, you identified the activities you could use as emotional, mental, and physical rest. Are there any of the activities from the Rest Test on your own list? Any you'd like to add to your Rest Bank?

What Isn't Rest?

In identifying your restful activities, you might also find some clues as to what you don't consider restful. There will be, I'm sure, some activities that you currently do in your leisure time that aren't particularly enjoyable or end up causing you more stress. In my opinion, one thing stands out as not being listed as "restful" by the Rest Test participants: social media.

The questionnaire for the Rest Test was administered in 2015 and, though the number of people owning smartphones has increased since then,[7] many were likely to have had access to a world of entertainment in their pockets as they were answering questions about their most restful, calming activities. Yet doomscrolling (bingeing on negative news) through Instagram reels doesn't feature on their list. Because, if we're being truthful, social media sites aren't relaxing.

You probably know that platforms use an algorithm to show you content that you're likely to engage with. These sites want your time and they want your energy, so they'll prioritize videos and posts that you'll interact with over the things you originally signed up for: connection with friends and the people who share your interests. The content you end up seeing is designed to instigate high-energy emotions rather than low-energy ones—if you're angry, you'll engage and reply; if you're excited, you'll share with others; if you're inspired, you'll watch, read, want more. Social media sites, in effect, have achieved the monetization of energy.

It may be that you follow accounts for the calm, relaxing content they share, but I'm not confident that's how you rack up hours of screen time daily. I still struggle to put down my phone at times when I should be resting, and even when I do, I'm thinking about taking a picture for Instagram or crafting a post about why rest is good for you. I have learned how to create better habits involving my phone, though, and we'll discuss these in chapter 12. Essentially, scheduling non-phone and phone time stops me from thinking that I absolutely have to post/scroll/watch *now* because I know I can do everything I want to do later, once I'm well rested. I also try to put my phone out of reach during non-phone activities, because I know willpower is an unnecessary drain on my energy.

Procrastination—using social media or any other activity—is not a form of rest. You may think that the time you spend avoiding a task is rest from said task, but it's likely that you're using that energy in other ways and berating yourself while doing so. The very nature of procrastination means that it causes extra stress and worry, now and later. Sometimes, procrastination is a good indication of needing to rest, as it can occur when you're not confident you have the energy or ability to fully take on a task. We'll talk more about procrastination in chapter 9 but remember that you need to allow yourself rest while also being strict about when you have done enough resting. A better relationship with energy use and rest can only help you avoid time spent procrastinating.

Variation Is Key

As with the way you use your energy, there can be too much of a restful thing. When you rely upon the same restful activities, you may find their restorative ability impacted. If you always listen to music when you work or drive your car, you might not agree that it should be listed as a restful activity. If you spend a lot of time daydreaming, you might find yourself more prone to ruminating over worries and anxieties. Watching TV can be relaxing, tranquilizing even, according to Claudia Hammond, one of the Rest Test's psychologists.[8] But overindulge and it may no longer be an enjoyable way to spend an evening.

Though restful activities can be goal-driven, like finishing a book, exercising for a race, or knitting a jumper, it's good to have a break from goal pursuit. If you're tempted to "optimize" your rest so that you can still feel like you're achieving something, you're still holding onto the belief that the only worthwhile way to spend energy is if it results in productivity.

While pacing helps stop the boom-and-bust pattern of a life run by your teleoanticipatory brain, sometimes you need to actively reject the need for a *telos* at all. A *telic* activity is one that has a set end point, but to stop and rest can require an *atelic* activity, one that is done for its own sake and not to reach a certain end. Consider walking just to explore and take in nature, rather than making your ten thousand daily steps. Make messy, unattractive art just to see the way the paint mixes together. Play for fun, not to teach or learn. Go out with your friends and enjoy yourself without guilt.

To be without a goal can be uncomfortable initially. If you've spent most of your adult life always striving for something, you've likely never stopped finding reasons for what you do. Make the discomfort part of the experience. See how it feels to be idle, to conserve, to rest.

Protecting Rest

Prioritizing rest makes sense on paper, but in practice it's difficult to dedicate time to activities that recharge your energy. When you're being pressured to use energy, whether by the people around you or your own inner voice, rest can feel selfish and even irresponsible.

When you do rest, you might be tempted to pick up your phone. There, you'll find the people who "work hard, play hard," the mothers taking their children to every extracurricular class under the sun, the gym-goers who post their daily workouts with the hashtag #NoPainNoGain. Everyone else will appear to be using their energy with no regard for rest or downtime, and it'll make it that much harder for you to stick to your slower, more manageable pace of life.

You don't need me to tell you that the lives we see on social media are an illusion, a retelling of only the best bits of the story, smoothed out and exaggerated. That doesn't really make it any easier to stop comparing yourself to the fictional characters that bear your friends' names and faces.

Setting—and sticking to—boundaries when it comes to your own energy will feel unnatural at first. It'll take conscious effort and energy to resist your inclination to always be "on," always be at your kids' beck and call, to say yes when your boss offers you extra shifts. Choosing to rest is easy when you're on vacation and the expectations of you are low, but at home, when the household tasks are literally in front of your face, it's much harder to maintain a balance of rest and activity.

In these instances, it's important to be kind to yourself. Don't make resting another thing you have to be perfect at. If, in the beginning, all you can manage is a five-minute walk away from your desk, that's fine. In Part Three, you'll design a pace of life that supports the building of good habits from small actions to lasting behavioral change.

You'll also likely compare yourself to your pre-pacing, boom-and-bust way of powering through without stopping to rest. If a particular life event has led you to start pacing—getting ill, taking on too much at work, becoming a parent—you'll also be tempted to compare the energy you have now to the way you felt before the change. But spend too long looking backward, or sideways, and you'll miss out on what's in front of you.

As you become more aware of how activities impact your energy levels, you'll find it easier to know when to be strict with your rest and when to be flexible. If you plan to read for half an hour each night, but your children want your help with their homework or your friends want to go out for a drink, you're able to reassess your feelings of energy and decide which path to take. If you're confident you can postpone your rest, reschedule it and choose an activity. But you can also choose to set your kids down in front of a YouTube video that explains the Pythagorean theorem, because you know you're out of mental energy for the day; or text your friend to say you'll join them next time. Your own health deserves as much respect as your social life or your children's grades.

> "Don't make resting another thing you have to be perfect at."

TASK

In Part One, you developed a Rest Bank of activities that you could use after exerting emotional, mental, or physical energy. Now, choose one of each type to take out as a "free trial" in the same way you've picked better diet and sleep habits to experiment with. Try to include variation and be wary of assigning a *telos* to each activity—rest for rest's sake is worthy of your time.

5 Principles of Rest

1. Life on Earth evolved to conserve energy wherever possible, yet society now sees busyness as the most desirable trait. Does your aversion to rest stem from the belief that to conserve energy is to be lazy?

2. You have to establish a good relationship with rest to allow yourself the time to recharge. Starting small, introduce some restful activities into your daily life, and really try to notice how they make you feel. In the beginning, taking time out might make you uncomfortable, or you'll find your mind can't stop thinking about work or chores. As resting becomes more habitual, you'll find it easier to enjoy the opportunities

to recharge, and you'll notice the difference in your overall energy and productivity.

3. Even if you think you already know which activities will suit you and your lifestyle best, it may be worth trialing some different options over the next few weeks. You might be surprised by the things that offer you a break from exerting mental energy or that help inspire lower-energy emotions.

4. Procrastination is not rest. If you're engaging in a restful activity but feeling guilty about not working, or are criticizing your own choices, you're using more energy, not recharging what you've already spent.

5. Respect your rest. Set boundaries for energy use and know when to be flexible about crossing them and when to be strict. Don't put off rest so long that your body is forced to make the decision for you and you find yourself back in a boom-and-bust pattern.

eight

Assess

~~~~~~~~~

Finding Your Vital Pace

NOW THAT YOU HAVE at least two weeks of your pacing diary, you can begin to work out where your energy is currently going and where it might be reduced in your new pace of life. You might be able to notice where you're booming and busting, across your day, week, and long-term activity.

A boom-and-bust pace of life can take many forms. You might overload your morning and then see an afternoon crash in energy levels, or you might spend all your energy during the day at work and find that every evening you are exhausted, unable to engage with the people around you or the hobbies you once loved. Your boom-and-bust pattern might present itself in weekdays of high energy and activity, followed by weekends of sleeping in, eating poorly, avoiding exercise and socializing. You may even see a boom-and-bust in your productivity at work, where a large project deadline gives you the energy to keep going until the very last minute. When you can finally celebrate the project's completion, you feel an overwhelming tiredness—the weight lifted from your shoulders doesn't offer relief; it reveals how small you feel when it's taken away. Or you may see that you're using a lot of emotional energy, day in, day out, with little opportunity for emotional rest.

If you have ME/CFS or long COVID, you may notice that even a single activity—the "boom" of your day—is causing a "bust" and increasing your symptoms, including pain, brain fog, and fatigue. Your pacing diary may reveal some surprising drains on your energy: I was shocked when I first noticed that standing still for any length of time had such a dramatic effect on my symptoms, evidenced by the surge in pain and weakness I had in my legs following any attempt at cooking or cleaning.

But I couldn't avoid all standing. I couldn't afford to pay someone to make all my meals or clean my home from top to bottom. There will be things you've identified as triggers for symptoms, or causing your boom-and-bust feelings of fatigue, that you can't simply stop doing. How, then, do you design a new pace of life around them?

In pacing, the beginning of any new pace starts with a calculation of the amount of energy you *have* to spend each day. In the management of ME/CFS, the amount of activity that a person can do without making symptoms worse is called the "baseline." But I like to refer to it as the vital pace. Baseline implies this activity is the least amount possible, and as you know by now, less isn't always better. Some will set their baseline far too low, but many will do the opposite and aim for an unrealistically high amount of activity each day. When I was first taught to pace, I did the latter. My expectations were too high, reflecting what I wanted my body to be able to tolerate rather than what it actually could. I resented my baseline. Who wants to be at the bottom, doing the bare minimum?

The vital pace is not the least amount; it's the requisite amount. It's the day-to-day spending of your energy based on your experience of fatigue, available energy, and essential activity. Instead of booming and busting, the vital pace sets a stable line of energy expenditure from which you can gradually build up, but one that you can also drop back to if need be without falling further into a bust.

"The beginning of any new pace starts with a
calculation of the amount of energy you have
to spend each day."

It can be a good idea to return to your vital pace in times of unexpected change—for example, if you catch a cold or get pregnant. While your body fights off the flu (or begins preparations to carry a baby for the next nine months), your energy levels will be altered. At this stage, it can be easy to fall back into a boom-and-bust lifestyle if you don't adjust your pace accordingly. By returning to your vital pace, you give yourself the chance to recover or to reflect on the best pace for your life going forward (your priorities for energy expenditure might have changed!). Then, when you feel confident that you can increase your activity, you begin pacing up again. This process is often easier and quicker than it was previously, because you've allowed yourself the period of rest and convalescence.

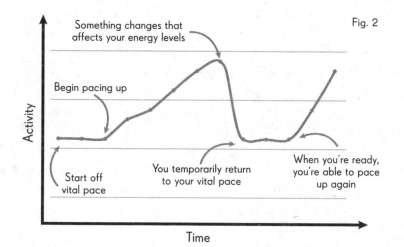

When you've been pushing yourself to the very limit of your energy levels for a long time, it's hard to believe there's any other way to live. Your plate is overloaded because it *has* to be, because everything you do is absolutely essential and can't be done by anyone else, right?

I know it feels that way. You wouldn't have gotten to where you are now without believing that it was necessary. I'm certain that there is a justifiable reason for everything you do, in every activity listed in your pacing diary. Clothes must be washed, food must be cooked, emails must be answered. You must be available at all times to help those around you who have come to rely on you, whether that's your boss, your customers, your friends, or your family.

Here's the toughest part of pacing: It will always be possible to do more than your pace of life. Your company will demand more of your time and energy, your kids will always benefit from more of your attention, you can always study more and strive for higher grades. In order to pace yourself, you'll have to acknowledge that you'll never be able to control these external pressures—though they do subside once the people in your life see that your new pace is here to stay—and be confident in the one thing you do have authority over: your knowledge of your own energy levels and the things that will knock them off balance.

This is where your vital pace becomes crucial. Once you've established the amount of energy and activity that is essential in your life, you'll soon see how much energy you have left each day to put toward your goals and your happiness.

The concept of a baseline of energy, or the vital pace, I feel is best described by a person with ME/CFS who was quoted in a 1999 paper on pacing: "I used to take two steps forward and three steps back, and now I take one step at a time."[1] Once you've established your vital pace, you'll feel confident in adjusting your stride, taking bigger steps, and using your energy to achieve your goals.

Defining Your Essential Activities

Your vital pace needs to include the activities that are absolutely essential and unavoidable to your day-to-day life, but will require you to be quite strict when it comes to deciding what these tasks actually are. You'll also have to rethink how and when you'll complete these activities, with a new focus on reducing the energy that they demand.

First, you'll need to go through your pacing diary and list all the activities that you do regularly—in other words, more than three times a week. Next, you'll need to work out whether each activity is essential to the next two weeks of your life.

Before you're tempted to put everything as "essential," really think about whether there are activities that could be postponed or reduced. After two weeks, provided your vital pace has been set right and you haven't felt any worse, you can start to add things back in— though the chances are you'll realize many of the activities you thought you needed to do are actually superfluous or exaggerated.

The most obvious activities to be included in your vital pace are those that satisfy a biological or physiological need. This includes things like making and eating food, sleeping, and resting. Any activity you need to undertake for a health reason, like taking medication or going for a treatment, should be included here, too.

What else, beyond these "basic" needs, counts as essential activity? When you consider this question, it's likely that you have a lot of factors to think about. You probably can't give up work for two weeks to remove those activities, nor can your children skip school so you don't have to make the school run (though that might make the energy demands of your day even higher, if you spend it trying to keep them entertained!). Then there is your weekly catch-up with friends, the class you take on Monday evenings, not to mention the housework and your exercise routine . . . everything on your current schedule seems important, I know.

Think of the next two weeks as a chance to pause: a period of convalescence after the exhausting experience of booming and busting for so long. Whittle down your activities to the really, *really* essential tasks, knowing that everything else can wait for a little while.

"Think of the next two weeks as a chance to pause: a period of convalescence after the exhausting experience of booming and busting for so long."

At Work or in Education

If you're in employment or studying, consider which activities you currently spend energy on that aren't part of your assigned workload. Not every work activity is essential. If you're a lawyer, turning up to court would be essential, but sitting in a meeting that will be summarized in an email later might not be. If you're a student, attending extra lectures or joining academic societies will look good on your résumé, but it's not a requirement for gaining your degree.

In my activity list, researching and interviewing scientists for articles are essential for my job, while replying to emails is generally not essential and could be postponed for a couple of weeks using an out-of-office message, with the caveat that I should be texted or called about anything urgent.

You might have taken on extra responsibilities informally, doing more in the hopes of getting a pay increase or a better graduate job later down the line. What would happen if you were to postpone these tasks until after you've established a sustainable vital pace?

Of course, you'll probably want to explain to your colleagues why you've suddenly stopped, but if they're being worked as hard as you are, I expect they'll understand why you're lightening your load temporarily to help your health and productivity in the long run. You may also need to have a conversation with your manager about this tactic to avoid being accused of "quiet quitting." You can explain that your actions are helping you design a better work/life balance, which will help prevent exhaustion and burnout and ultimately be in the best interests of your company as much as yourself.

It is hard to reduce the effort you put into your job or education, especially if you've spent most of your life associating your worth with your output. You may think that because you hold career goals, it would be a sign of failure to stop pursuing them, even for just fourteen days. But you're more than deserving of a better pace of life, one that allows you to reach your goals without burning out and ruining your health or your social life. If the first step toward that pace requires a little discomfort, I think it's worth it.

When you've identified all the work-related tasks that definitely can't be postponed for two weeks, write them into a list somewhere. Later in this chapter, you'll look at ways to reduce the energy requirements of each activity before adding it into your vital pace.

Housework and Caring Responsibilities

How much of your daily energy is used cleaning up after yourself or others or making sure that the basic needs of your dependents are met? For many people, housework and caring responsibilities will use as much energy as a full-time job, if not more.

Again, it's important to consider whether all your activities here are essential, or if some are just preferable or taken to an extreme. Are there compromises that can be made, even if begrudgingly? Remember that your vital pace is only the baseline of your activity—in Part Three you'll introduce more back into your pace of life, which can include the things that you left out of your vital pace.

Obviously, you can't stop caring for others. Mouths need feeding and clothes need washing. But there are a lot of activities that people find themselves committed to, not because they need to do them, but because they feel they ought to keep their house in a particular way or are worried that they have to do XYZ to raise their kids properly.

You are the one who gets to set your standards when you are implementing your vital pace. You don't have to have a perfect, spotless home. You don't need to resolve every small squabble among your children, or pick up all the dirty dishes your roommates or family members leave about the living room. As important as it is to manage others' expectations while you're going at your vital pace, it's equally key that you relax your own requirements for your activity. Let the people around you use their own energy first, without you swooping in to save them the effort and expending more of yours.

Socializing and Self-Care

While you may be tempted to overestimate the number of work or caring activities that are essential, you're likely to undervalue the importance of the things you need to do for your own health and well-being. If asked to prioritize all the things you do, how low would you place the things you do for self-care? Are you more willing to cancel social plans to work late than you are to leave on time, knowing you'll return to the task tomorrow?

Good relationships are our most fundamental psychological need, after food, water, and safe shelter, according to psychologist Abraham Maslow.[2] When considering your essential activities, don't forget the importance of things that make you feel love and belonging. Make time in your vital pace for a daily, positive social activity. This doesn't have to take much of your energy—send a text to a friend, record a voice note and send it to a family member, or look through photographs from a fun social event to trigger positive memories.

We'll discuss this further in chapter 11, but it's important that your pace includes some activities for the sole purpose of being happy. Happiness and enjoyment affect our feelings of energy and fatigue, so a day that includes at least one fun activity will likely also contain the energy to complete essential activities. Again, this activity doesn't have to be energy intensive. It could be bundled into another one of your daily tasks: cooking with a loved one, playing a game with a child or animal, using the expensive shampoo that makes your hair smell nice all day.

Sometimes, implementing your vital pace can feel like your days have been restricted to only the most boring, unavoidable tasks.

That really shouldn't be the case. True, you may have stopped some of the things you did for fun in addition to all the excess demands you'd had placed on you, but your days should now be less exhausting. Instead of seeing a future of more work, more stress, and less energy, you'll be a step closer toward a better pace of life.

Reducing the Energy Cost of Activity

Once you have your list of activities that need to be included in your vital pace, you'll next need to work out ways to reduce their individual energy demands. Even if you haven't been able to get rid of any work-related tasks or still have a long list of essential activities at this stage, your vital pace won't be as hectic as the way you have been living up until now. There should be a way to limit the energy demand of many of the activities on your list.

I like to tackle the high-energy tasks first, as you stand to gain a lot more if you can make these activities even a little easier. There are a few different ways to lighten the load: You might lessen the energy cost by spreading an activity over a larger time frame, breaking up the activity with rest periods, extracting only the essential elements from the activity, or by delegating part or all of the activity.

- **Spreading the cost:** Society sees busyness as a status symbol. In a bid to become ever busier, we've begun rushing our activities. Under the guise of "effectiveness" and "productivity," we've all sought to save as much time and energy as possible, only to put those savings toward doing more activity. We'll talk more about this in chapter 12, but by now I hope you appreciate how the intense energy expenditure associated with a busy life leads to exhaustion, burnout, and poor health. As an example, rushing an activity that uses mental energy might "cost" you more energy because it means you're more likely to make mistakes, which you'll later have to correct, and can increase your feelings of stress, using emotional energy.

Consider whether any of your essential activities could be slowed down to reduce their energy demand. What if you spent a little longer—even just ten minutes more—enjoying your breakfast, instead of wolfing it down and chucking the dirty dish into the sink? Would you make a healthier choice, get some more time with your kids, or have a peaceful moment in solitude before your stressful day starts?

- **Breaking up:** You now understand the importance of rest, but have you fully implemented what you learned in chapter 7? When we begin pacing, we tend to slot restful activities into our day *after* we've done an energy activity. If we're feeling in the zone with a task, or trying to resist distraction or procrastination, we're inclined to reserve our rest until the task is done. But the high-energy need of some activities can be lessened by putting small rest breaks into the activity. Some people use the Pomodoro Technique, which separates tasks into twenty-five-minute blocks with rest periods of five to ten minutes in between.[3] Others have tried the 52/17 Rule, which recommends that every fifty-two minutes of focused mental work is followed by seventeen minutes of rest.[4] For people with ME/CFS and long COVID, it's thought that rest breaks need to be much more frequent in order to prevent post-exertional malaise: Take a break after every three to fifteen minutes of activity. Are there any activities on your list that would benefit from being broken up? When you're tackling a big assignment or helping your children with their homework, can you resist the temptation to just power through and instead take short breaks that allow you to reflect on what you've done without the pressure of having to turn your thoughts into something worth a grade?

- **Compromising:** You've already identified that your activity is essential, but can you distill the activity down to the specific action needed to reach that benefit? What aspects of your activity are nonessential? I've classed walking the dog as essential because it gives me some light exercise and brings me closer to nature, which I know has a huge benefit to my well-being. And, obviously, it is essential for my dog! However, I might now consider these benefits individually. Is there a way I could get light exercise without spending as much energy? Would standing still in nature have a similar benefit? Can I provide the exercise for my dog another way, playing indoors or . . .

- **Delegating:** Is there someone else who can complete the activity and provide the benefit? This won't be possible for all tasks, but in my example, my husband and I can take turns walking the dog, or I could ask a friend to help, or, if finances allowed, "contract out" the activity to a professional dog-walker. Delegating your activity might not always cost money: You could trade the task with another, lower-energy activity undertaken by a member of your household or a colleague at work. Key here, though, is not to turn the action of delegating into just another energy expenditure. Wherever possible, make sure your communication is clear and that you're delegating effectively. If the person taking on your task is constantly returning with questions, or using up your energy in other ways, your delegating hasn't been effective. Equally, if I stress about *how* my husband walks the dog— whether he does it the way I would, whether he'll get her lost or dirty, and so on—then I'm not really saving myself any energy. When moving at your vital pace, certain concessions will need to be made. You can't hold yourself, or anyone else, to standards that will upset your vital pace. Besides, my husband has only lost the dog once, so far . . .

· · ·

If, after making these changes to your activities, you still find your vital pace to be taking up too much of your energy, you may want to try deferring certain activities. One of the hardest parts of living with an energy-limiting illness is having to let go of things you were once able to do without a second thought. But if you do have to remove activities in order to manage your vital pace, remember that these are deferred and not deleted. Let them go for now, knowing that if they're really important, you can work them into your new pace of life a little later down the line.

In Part Three we'll look at what's known as pacing up: adding in activity above our vital pace to gradually increase the amount of energy we have each day. Nobody wakes up and decides to run a marathon. They need to practice increasing their distance over time. Their muscles improve, their tolerance increases, until one day they manage the full 26.2 miles. This happens with cognitive effort—it's been termed "learned industriousness."[5] This will happen with your vital pace, too. Over time, you'll be able to add more activity into your days without sending your pace back into a boom-and-bust.

> "If you do have to remove activities in order to manage your vital pace, remember that these are deferred and not deleted."

Committing to Your Vital Pace

Now that you've established the activities that will make up your vital pace, it's time to commit to sticking with them for at least the next two weeks. Don't be tempted to wait until the right time to start your vital pace—there is no perfect time. Whatever pressures are on you currently, you can't wade through them to reach a point in the future when the stress and demands will be less and you feel comfortable reducing your activity down to your vital pace. More pressures will come: new projects at work, classes to take the kids to, events to attend, and people to network with. You'll reach your breaking point sooner than you'll find the "right" time to slow down.

When you do implement your vital pace, you may initially be met with some internal and external resistance. It'll feel uncomfortable for a while, saying no to things you'd previously have taken on. In comparison to the thrilling highs of the boom-and-bust cycle, your vital pace might seem mundane, boring even. You could be tempted to increase quickly, adding in new activities before you've had a chance to really test your vital pace. But rushing into doing more could put you back into the cycle. Remember that you will be designing your new pace of life in Part Three, crafting it from the goals you have and the things that bring you joy, to avoid exhaustion and burnout. Trust that you will be able to do more in the future.

It may be hard for the people around you to understand why you've let go of some of your previous habits or responsibilities. They might still believe that doing more is always better, that to turn down work in favor of rest is a sign of weakness or failure. If you feel like you have the energy to explain to them why you're moving at a slower pace, you can—but you're under no obligation. What matters right now is your own health and well-being. If you decide later that one of your goals is to help others design a new pace of life, then you can find a way to take steps in that direction.

In the meantime, if there are tasks that they view as essential but don't feature in your vital pace, you can suggest that they take them on, with any of the energy adjustments you learned on [pages 98–100].

The Vital Pace in Moderate-to-Severe Cases

For people with very limited energy, whether due to severe ME/CFS, long COVID, depression, or any other reason, the "basic" activities of eating, sleeping, and maintaining hygiene may be all that can be included in the vital pace. Trying to do any more than this can lead to the boom-and-bust cycle of energy expenditure followed by extreme fatigue. In these instances, a vital pace that is set too high can aggravate symptoms and make even the most basic of tasks, like eating and drinking, difficult and painful. Many people I know living with severe ME/CFS can only get by thanks to the help and support of friends and family, and if they're lucky, a good doctor, adjustments at work, and financial aid.

When I was at my worst, I would've been classed as moderate-to-severe, and I couldn't leave my home until I'd spent a few months gradually adding in small activities to my vital pace, or "pacing up," which we'll look at more closely in Part Three.

TASK

Schedule the activities in your vital pace across the next two weeks. Wherever you find gaps in your days, include activities from your Rest Bank that allow you to recharge emotional, mental, and physical energy. You could think of these weeks as a vacation from your boom-and-bust lifestyle, from which you'll return ready to pursue new activities and use your energy for your own happiness.

Read through Part Three of the book while you're completing your two-week vital pace. Any activities that weren't included in your pace will be considered again in chapter 13, when you'll be able to schedule them back into your design for your new pace of life if you choose.

You can download a printable PDF of a schedule for your vital pace from amyarthur.co.uk or map out your activity using your current diary method.

5 Principles of Finding Your Vital Pace

1. The vital pace serves as a baseline of activity that you can build upon, pacing up as and when you have more energy. It isn't about doing the minimum, nor trying to cram as much activity into as small a time frame as possible.

2. Take the next two weeks to implement your vital pace. Consider it a period of convalescence, recovery from booming and busting for so long.

3. Really think about which tasks within your days can be postponed for the next two weeks. Only essential activities form part of our vital pace, though remember that socializing and resting are just as important as working.

4. Reduce the energy demand of the activities within your vital pace. You might do this by spreading them over a longer time period, breaking them up with small rest activities, compromising on the specific details of the task, or delegating the activity to someone else.

5. When you set your vital pace, you'll need to manage expectations and be prepared for some resistance, internally and from others. Feel confident about the decisions you've made, but acknowledge others' concerns—they likely hold themselves to the same or even higher standards that they're measuring you against.

part three
Design

"The curious paradox is that when I accept myself just as I am, then I can change."

—Carl Rogers, *On Becoming a Person*

NOW THAT YOU'VE established a good diet, quality sleep, and your vital pace, you can start thinking about any energy you have left and how you might like to use it. This part of the book will delve into the research that can help in the pursuit of your goals, the science of happiness and well-being, and your conceptions of time. You'll also learn how to craft good habits and break any bad ones.

Then, in chapter 13, you'll bring everything you've read together to design your new pace of life—one that allows you to do what you want in life and still maintain a balance of work and downtime, purpose and pleasure.

nine

The Pacing Lifestyle

PACING IS A LIFESTYLE, not a method or tool to implement once for immediate success. It requires behavioral and cognitive change, which, unfortunately, given its nature, takes effort. Change isn't easy, especially when the world around you stays the same, with its demands on your time and energy, its glorification of busyness, and rejection of rest.

By now, you've recognized that you have been living in a boom-and-bust cycle. Your relationship with energy is like a roller coaster: up when you're achieving, down when you're feeling exhausted.

In Part Two, you identified the ways in which you can support your energy by improving your sleep, diet, and rest. All that's left to do is to put your hand up, tell life you're stepping off the boom-and-bust roller coaster, and make a new route to follow. Right?

While you may feel you're ready to add more activity above your vital pace, it's important not to just jump back on the boom-and-bust roller coaster. It will be tempting to do so: You'll likely feel you have more spare energy than you've had in a long time. You may even be uncomfortable with having to hold back, seeing activities and opportunities pass by because they're not part of your vital pace. For now, try to resist the temptation to spend any spare energy. Instead, focus on setting up a lifestyle in which you will be able to do more and more over time, in what we call "pacing up," without getting back on the roller coaster.

The pacing lifestyle involves developing a mindset that gives you the confidence to make changes to the way you use your energy. You'll learn how to craft behaviors and routines that make pacing a habit. Most important, you'll want to establish an environment that encourages a better relationship with your energy and allows you to pace yourself even when the people around you demand your time and attention.

The Pacing Mindset

You already know that your current pace of life is exhausting you. Whether you're tired because you have a health condition or because you're stressed or burned out, one thing is true: The way you are spending your energy is unsustainable. You are depleting your energy day in, day out, expecting to fully recharge overnight and feel no ill effects. Sleep, while important, is no miracle cure. You cannot sleep your way off the roller coaster.

How, then, do you make significant and sustainable change so that you can avoid falling back into the boom-and-bust cycle? Part of this involves having what I refer to as a pacing mindset—an awareness of your own energy levels and confidence in your ability to work with them, rather than against them.

In chapter 4, we discussed making energy salient so that you can notice its impacts throughout your day. You could say you became "conscious of your incompetence" when it came to managing energy, though, and that's a natural starting point—whether you're learning a new language, playing a new sport, or trying a different way of living, you have to realize where you are currently to move upward.

The goal now is to become "unconsciously competent," so that pacing becomes almost second nature. After living with ME/CFS for over a decade, I would say I'm unconsciously competent most of the time, but I still have times where I misjudge an activity or find managing my energy levels is temporarily out of my hands while my body fights off a cold or flu.

This level of competence-without-thinking is only achieved by first being "consciously competent," or putting effort into implementing new habits that develop your competence. You'll identify these habits in the next section, but first you need to hold a mindset that gives you the best chance of choosing (and sticking to) the right changes and routine.

Your belief in your own ability and autonomy will have a big impact on how motivated you are to maintain your new pace of life.[1] This doesn't mean you'll always be motivated, as we'll discuss in a moment, but it does help foster a sense of confidence that will support you when the temptation to return to the boom-and-bust life comes calling.

Having a sense of autonomy means that you feel you have control over your own activities and that your day-to-day actions are in line with your overall goal (in this case, to have a better pace of life). This isn't always an easy thing to have—your activity and energy expenditure will be at the mercy of your financial situation, your home, the people around you. But within these demands, which sometimes feel like they're pulling you in opposite directions, there should be an element of autonomy. Some part of your energy each day should be reserved for your own use, even if it's only a small amount left after your vital pace. It may be that you have to adjust others' expectations of you, or compromise on things you've had in place for years, but your own autonomy is worth it.

Believing in your ability to do things well is one of the first things to deplete when you experience the emotional exhaustion that comes with burnout. Likewise, when you have a condition that limits your energy, it can feel like you have no ability at all, that your condition is what determines the outcomes of your actions.

Your emotional, mental, and physical states do affect your feelings of self-efficacy, which is the term that describes the confidence we have in our ability. But there are other factors that you can exert some control over to help bolster your self-efficacy, even when there are circumstances out of your hands.[2]

Of course, past experience can influence belief in your ability. If you've tried to get control over your own energy in the past, whether the outcome was positive or negative will probably affect how you feel about trying again now. But your self-efficacy is also impacted by other people's experience—living vicariously through another can actually help you feel better about your own chances of success. Knowing that people, myself included, have found a better pace of life will, I hope, help you see that it's possible.

Another contributor to self-efficacy is verbal persuasion, according to psychologist Albert Bandura, who first came up with a theory of self-efficacy in 1977.[3] Encouragement or discouragement can affect how you feel about your chances, and we'll look at these more closely in the pacing environment section.

It's also been suggested that you can build your self-efficacy through visualization—imagining what it'd be like to be successful in your goal to bring yourself closer to actually achieving it. In the final chapter, you'll use a schedule to visualize and design your new pace of life, which should make you realize it's a lot more attainable than you might think.

The final part of the pacing mindset is perseverance. Note that this does not mean "persist without rest" or "never make a mistake." You will make mistakes when you pace yourself. You'll misjudge the energy demands of an activity, or you'll slip unconsciously back into a boom-and-bust cycle when things happen, as they do, all at once, and you feel you have no choice but to give up some of your planned rest or happy activities. Writing this book affected my pace of life, and I had to make some adjustments to the design to accommodate the energy demands of the ever-looming deadline.

This is where the importance of establishing your vital pace comes in: When you experience setbacks, you'll be able to rely on your ability to revisit your pace. When time and life allow, once you're past whatever took up all your energy temporarily, you can return to chapter 8, and implement your vital pace again. Think of it as your constant: When you notice your control over your energy slipping, know that you can take it back with your vital pace.

Setbacks will happen: They are not failures. Yet they will still feel uncomfortable, frustrating, even painful, especially if they come from post-exertional malaise. What's important, in the face of a setback, is that you preserve some sense of self-efficacy. That you appreciate and accept that this is temporary.

You may want to resist acknowledging the setback, try to push through it and pretend like all is okay. Don't. Notice the signs of emotional, mental, and physical exhaustion and implement what you've learned from this book. Don't let yourself fall so far you end up in a "bust."

"Knowing that people, myself included, have found a better pace of life will, I hope, help you see that it's possible."

The Pacing Habit

At the moment, it may seem like pacing will take a lot of conscious effort. But lessons from behavioral science can help you design a pace of life that will stick, even in times when your motivation is low and the temptation to waver is high. This means making pacing a habit so that, over time, your ability to monitor your energy and adjust the balance of your activity becomes almost second nature.

Learning how to properly craft habits will help you turn any "free trials" you took out in Part Two into well-established behaviors in your new pace of life. It will also help you reduce any energy-draining habits you've identified so that you have the best chance possible of pacing up to reach longer-term goals.

There are some great books on the subject of habits, each with their own slightly different take on the psychology of behavioral change. Which, essentially, is what you're trying to do when you begin your new pace of life. You've got the knowledge of energy and fatigue, you've got competence and belief in yourself. Now, you need to make some physical changes.

The essence of habit theory is that repeated behavior when attached to a trigger becomes a consistent and often unconscious action. This applies to good habits and bad, and it's what you need to understand if you're going to reduce some of the things that drain your energy and implement new routines to help you use it more wisely.

Habits are formed over time, the result of repeated experience responding in a certain way. The first time you were taught to brush your teeth, you probably put up a bit of resistance. The next day, when the time came to clean your teeth *again*, you weren't any more excited by the prospect. It might've taken quite a bit of time, effort, and cajoling for you to form the habit you (it is hoped) have now of brushing your teeth twice a day. The trigger or prompt for brushing your teeth in the morning might be that you pass your bathroom on your way downstairs or that you always keep a toothbrush in the shower or simply the reinforced routine of "get up, clean teeth, have breakfast."

In order to start a new habit, you have to identify two things: the behavior that you want to perform and the starting prompt that'll encourage you to enact the behavior.

Starting Behaviors

Some of the new habits you might like to start could be performing rest activities during the day or checking in with your energy levels when you wake up in the morning. In the next chapter, when you identify some goals for your new pace of life, you'll also want to craft habits that form the steps toward these goals. For now, though, I'd suggest you choose one of the bits of advice from Part Two that you've yet to try and use it to craft a new habit that will help you implement what you've learned.

Generally, the advice in starting a new habit suggests that initially your desired behavior should be:

- Small
- Low energy
- Enjoyable or rewarding

In his book *Tiny Habits*, behavioral scientist BJ Fogg recommends starting with the smallest possible version of your habit.[4] If your goal is to floss your teeth every day, start by flossing just one tooth. After a while—unfortunately, there's no hard and fast rule about how long it takes to form a habit, with studies suggesting anywhere between 15 to 254 days![5]—flossing one tooth will turn into two, then three, then you'll have your new habit ingrained.

When it comes to defining small pacing behaviors, think about the long-term habit you want to establish, then ask yourself, what would doing half of that habit look like? Then, what's half of that? And half of that? Obviously, this can go on forever, but you'll reach a point where you feel like your behavior is at its smallest (you can't floss half a tooth!).

Say you hope to find time for emotional rest in your day, as you've realized emotional exhaustion is a big contributor to your overall fatigue. You've identified the activity that you could use for this rest as being physical exercise. The hour-long yoga class at your nearby gym would be a great activity, but joining in would require lots of things: a membership, a yoga mat, a free hour in your busy schedule, not to mention the motivation to actually go. But what's half of that class? A thirty-minute YouTube video? Half it, and half again, until you get down to the smallest behavior: one yoga pose held every morning.

The behavior should also be low in energy. If it demands too much effort, it's going to be difficult to repeat regularly. My advice is to consider yourself at your most tired when designing your habit—if it's still possible to do at this point of low energy, it's something that can turn into a consistent behavior.

Your new habit shouldn't just be easy to perform; it should also be easy to access. Perhaps you want to implement a step toward your goal of eating more healthily. Your milestone might be to "eat five vegetables every day." You've broken this down into a small behavior of a handful of carrot sticks with lunch. But when you're rushed off your feet, trying to focus on your next big project, or keeping the kids occupied during school vacations, will you stop to peel a carrot and chop it up, or will you reach for the packet of chips?

Making this behavior more easily accessible might involve removing chips from your shopping list (or, if the other people in your household would complain, buying ones you don't like but everyone else does). It might also mean spending some time one day, when you do have a bit more energy, preparing five portions of carrot sticks that you can eat on the go during the week.

Finally, your new, small, easy behavior should be enjoyable or rewarding, or ideally both. If you hate yoga or carrots, perhaps you haven't found the right habit to help you reach your goals. Even if you don't have any strong adverse feelings toward starting your day with downward dog or munching on midday carrot sticks, without enjoyment or a reward, when something unexpected pops up to demand your attention and energy, your new habit will be one of the first things to be sidelined.

I much prefer to design habits that involve some enjoyment. As you'll see in chapter 11, happiness has a big impact on feelings of energy and effort. If you can, tie an element of pleasure into your new habit. If you can practice your yoga outside in the garden or while on FaceTime with a friend, you might get more enjoyment out of the practice. If the carrots you eat are ones you've grown or you bought from the local farmer, you might feel they have a sense of purpose attached to them, which boosts happiness (okay, maybe I'm reaching here, but you get the point!). You could also try "temptation bundling," which involves attaching something fun to a less enjoyable activity, like listening to an audiobook while using the treadmill at the gym.[6]

Some habits won't be enjoyable. That doesn't mean they're not worthwhile. In these cases, find ways to reward yourself. Make the reward specific and exclusive. "Specific" means you've set the reward in advance, while "exclusive" means this reward is reserved solely for the completion of your habit. If you eat ice cream every evening, it won't feel like much of a reward after your weekly French lesson.

Starting Prompts

Once you've identified your small, easy, enjoyable behavior, you need to pick a prompt that will initiate the start of your new habit. Don't rely on motivation or memory. Motivation will come and go, while your memory will become easily distracted by all the other things you have to hold in your mind as you go about your day.

If you try to just remember to eat your carrot sticks every day, there will be plenty of times where you've been distracted by a lunchtime meeting or last night's leftovers, and before you know it, you've only completed your habit once in two weeks.

You may think you'll be consistently motivated to perform your new behavior, but that, I'm afraid to say, is wishful thinking. Motivation has its own boom-and-bust pattern, appearing when the reward for an action is unusually high or the deadline for an action is imminent. Although having motivation has been tied to feelings of energy, it's also one of the first things to go when you start feeling tired.[7]

The truth is you don't need motivation to act. Sure, it helps, but if you sit around and wait for it, it's unlikely to appear. If you can find ways to prompt action without it, you'll be able to start your habit now and reap the benefits if motivation does show up later.

According to scientist Dr. Julia Ravey, a good cue for starting a new habit should be specific, visible, and sacred.[8] Turn "in the morning" to "as soon as I get out of bed" for a more specific prompt to perform your one yoga pose. A visible cue could be to leave your yoga mat in view of your bed, or to make your wake-up alarm the start of an instructional video. For a cue to be sacred, it means it should only be tied to this particular habit. If you try to tag too many new behaviors on to "getting out of bed," you might find you only perform one or two before you get fed up or, worse, you'll stay in bed until time constraints mean you can't do any of them.

I'd also add that your prompt should be something positive, because the halo effect means that we generally form associations between things based on the weight of the first impression.[9] If you pick "after taking your daily vitamin" as your prompt but you really hate swallowing pills, this dislike will spill over into whatever habit you've attached to it.

There is an element of trial and error with finding the right prompt for your new habit, as people are rarely able to anticipate successfully what works and what doesn't.[9] Experiment with your habits to see what suits you and your needs best.

Breaking Habits

You're in luck: Everything you've just learned about forming habits also applies to breaking habits. If you can pick out your behaviors and prompts for a bad habit, you can get in the way of your own action.

You may have already identified some of your existing habits that have impacted your energy levels. These might be linked to things we talked about in chapter 5 in relation to your diet, or in chapter 6 on sleep. Or, your habit might be one of avoidance—

neglecting your rest on a regular basis, staying at work late because you don't want to go home, leaving difficult assignments until the very last minute. These are all repeated behaviors associated with a trigger that have become a consistent action, and so meet the definition of a habit.

Sometimes it's easier to break a bad habit by replacing it with a good one. This works in most cases when your action relates to your diet or sleep, when it's obvious what the good version of your habit might be.

Avoidance habits are trickier. They can't be swapped easily: It might take a bit of effort to make your home situation more welcoming, or to rid yourself of the notion that rest is "unproductive" and a "waste of time." So, you procrastinate. And that's a habit, too.

> "Sometimes it's easier to break a bad habit by replacing it with a good one."

Procrastination

There are many, many reasons why you might procrastinate—and it's likely that you do, at least on the odd occasion. As many as one in five people worldwide are chronic procrastinators,[11] and this problematic behavior can have serious consequences: putting off doctor's appointments until illnesses become severe, jeopardizing careers because projects are delayed, hurting your own self-image and increasing the risk of mental health problems and anxiety,[12] among others.

If you know that procrastination *now* will lead to harm *later*, why do you still feel the desire to delay? There are a few reasons.[13] Perhaps you have a present-emotion bias, in which your feelings at this point in time seem much more important than the feelings of future-you, so you opt for what's easy or enjoyable now and save the effortful tasks for later. Maybe you perceive the value of the outcome to be so low it's not worthwhile, or that your belief in your own ability to achieve is poor. The deadline for completing your action might be far away or undefined or even nonexistent. Then, the allure of other distractions might outweigh any potential positives from the task at hand.

Whatever the reason, when the urge to procrastinate surfaces, it can be very hard to push it away. But procrastinating has an impact on our energy levels. We may think we're saving energy by putting off what is more effortful, but we'll spend extra energy in the long run.

The thing you do while you're procrastinating will use energy, and you'll still have to use your energy to perform the task anyway, except you'll be under more stress (and likely to fatigue faster as a result). The guilt and unease you feel while you're procrastinating will use emotional energy, too. Over time, procrastination can deplete our ability to handle difficult things, meaning tasks will demand more energy of us.

But you can treat procrastination as you would any other habit. The desire to procrastinate serves as the prompt to enact the procrastination behavior. The more you procrastinate, the more concretely this habit forms. It's a tough habit to break, to be sure, and I can't say I never procrastinate (I definitely have while writing this chapter, even!), but I do have more control over when and how I spend my energy by using some of the tricks from behavioral science.

The first thing to do is to look at your procrastinating behaviors. Are there things you usually do while procrastinating? Mine include going on my phone, watering the plants, and washing up. Note how none of these activities are "bad" ways to spend my energy. I don't want to stop doing those things, but I do want to do them of their own accord, not when I'm trying to avoid doing something else. These behaviors fit the description for habits, in that they're relatively small, low-effort, and enjoyable (if I'm on my phone) or rewarding (tending to plants that I've grown or by making me feel like my environment is clean and tidy).

One way to limit procrastination is by making these behaviors larger, harder, less enjoyable, and unrewarding. I could keep my phone well away from my desk (harder) or delete my social media apps (less enjoyable). I could do the washing up before I start work, removing it as a possible behavior altogether.

Then, look to your procrastination prompts. What usually triggers the desire to procrastinate? Is it when you feel stuck with a particular problem, or when the task is below a certain level of enjoyment? Do you procrastinate on specific parts of your job—replying to emails, sending out posts, writing reports—more than others?

You can then try to alter these prompts by tweaking the situation itself. This might mean adding an element of enjoyment ("going through my inbox is boring, but I can do it while listening to my favorite album") or reframing the emotion attached to the task ("I hate writing references" becomes "writing references is boring but tolerable").

Or you could use these prompts to form new habits. You might be able to come up with some small, easy, and relevant behaviors that you can use as a response to each trigger when it arises. For example: I'm always tempted to procrastinate when I get to a certain stage of any journalistic assignment, when I've done the research, but I can't figure out how to begin the article. The introduction of any article has to draw the reader in and it's this pressure that makes me want to opt for an easier task, like dealing with my dirty dishes.

But my new behavior in response to the prompt within my brain of "time to write the intro" has become: List everything I think needs to be said at the beginning of the piece. A list is small, easy, and yet still useful. It gets words on the page. I can move onto the body of the article and then come back to finish the introduction later.

There is one form of procrastination that is difficult to resolve with habit alone. The desire to procrastinate can sometimes come from a place of fear or uncertainty. If you're feeling anxious about the task, or about your ability to complete it to the high standards you set for yourself, you'll be inclined to put it off. You may think that "future-you" will somehow be more capable or at least less uncertain. The fear of doing something badly—which, to the procrastinator, usually means "not perfectly"—can be paralyzing.

The only way I have found around this form of procrastination is to actively decide to do something poorly, because doing a task badly is better than not doing it. Every time, I'm surprised by how quickly this reframing quiets the urge to procrastinate. Sometimes, when I tell myself I'm allowed to start the first draft of an assignment with spelling mistakes, poorly strung-together paragraphs, and notes to add in references later, I end up with a rough version of a piece that isn't half bad. Knowing I've already done some of the legwork certainly makes starting the process again the following day a lot easier.

You will still procrastinate sometimes, and that's okay. Forgive yourself when it happens, as that might even help stop it from becoming a habit.[14]

The Pacing Environment

Any change is best undertaken in a supportive, comfortable environment. If you feel your new pace of life is threatened or if obstacles stand in your way, this might make it harder to turn behaviors into habits.[15]

Assuming you're able to access your basic needs of food and drink, sleep, safety, and security, what other aspects of your environment can affect your new pace of life? It's likely that the people around you will have something to say about any changes you're making, because, in fairness, they'll be affected, too.

When you change your priorities and how you allocate your energy, some of the people who have benefited, however unwittingly, from your boom-and-bust lifestyle might express resistance. Your boss, your colleagues, your friends, and your family will all notice a difference in your relationship with them. You might have already experienced some confrontation as you begin to implement your vital pace. The things that they find important might not have been at the top of your priority list. Some might've demanded an explanation as to why they're getting less (or more) of your energy than before.

Remember that the people around you haven't been privy to your own experience. They haven't carefully analyzed your energy expenditure, noticed your boom-and-bust pattern, or identified what makes you happy. To them, this change may be sudden and seemingly unwarranted. They need to be eased into your new pace of life just as much as you do.

It's frustrating when others don't understand your previous pain and suffering enough to appreciate your change of pace. But it's not always the case that they're simply not trying hard enough to understand. When someone is experiencing pleasure or otherwise going about life without experiencing anything truly unpleasant, it's much harder to understand the problems of others. They will underestimate the suffering, the pain, and the fatigue, not because they don't believe it but because their brain finds it difficult to recognize the depth of a situation so opposite to their own.[16]

The people in your life who feel empathy for your exhausted state may also have trouble showing it. Compassion is the motivation to alleviate the distress of another, but it can be extremely difficult for those around you to be compassionate when they don't understand the nature of your problems or how they can best help. They're likely conflicted about what to do, how much advice to offer, or when to resist acting so that your own resilience can grow.

The best way to help the people around you understand is to have an honest conversation about your new pace of life, the compromises you'll have to make, and how you'll support each other through any difficulties that arise.

On paper, pacing can seem simple: Plan for, and stick to, activity that uses your energy without exhausting you. But pacing in real life is much more complicated. You can't always prioritize your energy levels, nor avoid fatigue entirely. When others depend on your energy—whether they're family, friends, work colleagues, or customers—there will always be an element of negotiation as to who does which activities. If your day has taken its toll on your mental and physical energy, you cannot just assume that your partner will have the capacity to make dinner and put the kids to bed. But if you know that every week, on the days you go into the office instead of working from home, you'll be too tired to decide what to make for tea and then argue over who does or doesn't "fancy" eating that meal, a conversation in advance can help come up with a solution without using any more of your energy. Can you plan to have an easy meal that night of the week? Can you batch cook the weekend before, or have last night's leftovers for that meal?

Though you should set boundaries and stick up for your new pace of life, you also need to respect that your energy levels are no more important than those of your partner, your parents, your children. Your being more selective about how you use your energy doesn't mean you can choose how others should use theirs.

It's worth considering what your boundaries are before these conversations arise, as your judgment in the moment might be affected by your emotions and energy level.

When you do communicate your new pace to others, it's important to also reassure them of the things that are consistent—whether that's your love for your family, your dedication to your work, or the desire for health and longevity. For some, seeing you change your life may remind them of how stuck they feel in their own boom-and-bust cycle, or of their preconceptions of what success and "a life well lived" looks like.

As important as habits and boundaries are, flexibility and freedom are also crucial to the pacing lifestyle. Sometimes activities should be cherished, savored, rather than adopted into a routine as an ordinary habit. Appreciating the inconvenience of impromptu plans, even if they use more energy than you'd like, can lead to some of our happiest memories.

5 Principles of the Pacing Lifestyle

1. Holding a pacing mindset means having confidence in your ability to set your own pace and the agency to enact it. There are, of course, things out of your control, but you can still show respect for your own energy levels by making decisions that support them.

2. Know when and how to return to your vital pace: Use it as your safety net. If (or when) you find yourself heading toward another boom-and-bust pace of life, turn back to chapter 8 and implement what you can.

3. Building habits will help you turn the "free trials" you've found help your energy levels or reduce your feelings of fatigue into long-lasting lifestyle changes.

4. You can also use your new understanding of habits to help you reduce the unwanted actions that currently contribute to your feelings of fatigue. Remember that habits can be hard to break, especially if they've been kept up for a long time—manage your expectations when trying anything new.

5. As much as you can, try to surround yourself with people who support your new pace of life. This can take time and energy, as those who've known your old pace might struggle to understand why you've made some changes and may show some resistance. Reassure them of the solidity of your relationship, that you want them to be part of your new pace of life.

ten

Small Steps to Big Goals

SO FAR IN LIFE, your subconscious brain has largely set your pace. But the brain is unable to comprehend the vastness of human experience—the hundreds of months, tens of thousands of days, and millions of hours that we'll get to spend on this planet, all being well. It cannot set a consistent pace over such a variable, unimaginable length of time. So, it uses end points, or goals, to decide how we move forward.

This, you'll remember, is called teleoanticipation. It is the brain's ability to take a goal and break it down into small checkpoints, calculating how long and how much effort it'll take to reach the end. These calculations can be based on intrinsic or extrinsic factors. Your belief in your ability, your desire and motivation, and your fears about not realizing your goal all factor into your brain's teleoanticipatory calculations. The expectations of those around you, the pace at which others have reached similar goals, and the impact that achieving your goal will have on your environment, security, and social status will also dictate the pace your brain sets for you.

It's a natural and useful feature of the brain. In the short term, the brain needs to be able to calculate the time and energy a task will take because there are so many time- and energy-dependent activities in life. How could you cook a healthy, nutritious meal without being able to juggle multiple pans and cooking times? This day-to-day task management is often referred to as "executive function," and it relies on different areas of the brain communicating with one another, sending neural messages back and forth to generate plans, imagine and test their theory, and then physically execute them.

You also need to be able to plan and strive for long-term goals. You couldn't cook yourself a meal if you hadn't had the forethought to go food shopping on the weekend. You also couldn't cook if you hadn't made sure your bills were paid, that your oven or microwave worked, or that you had clean plates to eat off. When past-you was achieving these goals (setting up a direct debit to your energy company, loading the dishwasher), you weren't consciously thinking of a specific meal, completing your tasks for the sole purpose of making dinner on a Wednesday night. Rather, you were enacting routine habits in the service of an abstract goal. Your brain didn't need a specific goal to see the value in its pursuit.

Clearly, our brain is sometimes justified in setting the pace to achieve certain goals. But that doesn't mean we should give it free rein over all aspects of our life. As you've seen, making conscious dietary decisions can have a big impact on our health and well-being. Luckily, your brain is flexible—you can learn new information and adjust your pace.

What Is Your Destination?

In order to set your own pace, you need to figure out where you're heading. This means setting goals that are energy-conscious, motivating, and based in action, not outcome. This will be your main task for this chapter.

You've identified the imbalances concerning where you're currently spending your energy, but be wary of creating another imbalance when trying to correct your current pace. If, at the end of Part

Two, you realized that you were using too much energy at work and not putting enough into your relationships, it may be tempting to now put all the energy you have above your vital pace into your social life. If you did, you'd quickly find yourself on another boom-and-bust ride.

I find it helps to have a few goals at any one time, usually one for each of the three types of energy. This helps avoid letting any one type overwhelm your activities, while also preventing the detrimental effect of using too little energy. However, taking on too many goals at once risks another boom-and-bust pace, as you'll try to squeeze them all into your pace of life and likely leave rest out of the equation.

Just because you've identified a goal doesn't mean you have to start pacing toward it right away. You may have several goals in life, but there's no rule that says you have to be actively pursuing all of them to demonstrate how much you want them. When you only have so much time and energy available, you need to be selective about the goals you strive for. Spreading yourself too thin will, at best, mean that you never make meaningful progress in any of your goals, and at worst, it'll lead you to burnout and exhaustion.

Be flexible with your goals and reassess them regularly, ideally at the milestones along the way, which we'll discuss in a moment. It's natural for your goals to change as you and your situation change. You likely don't have the same goals you did when you were a teenager, nor will you have the same goals in retirement as you do now.

"In order to set your own pace, you need to figure out where you're heading."

Designing Your Goals

I cannot tell you exactly what your goals should be or what you should or shouldn't consider when setting them. What I will do is explain how your feelings of energy link to your goals and how, in turn, your goals affect your energy levels.

There are plenty of goal-setting methods to try, like making SMART goals (specific, measurable, achievable, relevant, and time-bound) or using the GROW model to identify your goal, reality, obstacles and options, and way forward. Some people swear by STD goals, an unfortunate name for objectives that are specific, time-bound, and difficult. Then there are ABC goals: achievable, believable, and committed. One large analysis of 141 studies in goal-setting and achievement suggests that "optimally, goals should be: difficult but achievable, set publicly, set face to face, set as a group goal, and set without drawing attention to goal commitment."[1]

A Google search reveals even more types of goals to be tried and tested, but ultimately, the best goal is one that works for you. Some books I'd recommend if you'd like a deeper exploration of the psychology of goal setting are in "Further Reading" at the end of this book.

In my experience, goals that aid pacing are:

- Energy-sustainable, allowing for natural dips and busy periods in life
- Energy-generating, in the form of renewing motivation
- Energy-conscious, so that our overall pace is manageable

It will help if you have one of your goals in mind as you read through this chapter. As an example, I'll refer to one of my own goals: to write a novel.

Energy-Sustainable: Consistency Over Outcome

When it comes to the outcome of goals, neuroscientist Dr. Julia Ravey writes in her brilliant book *Braintenance: A Scientific Guide to Creating Healthy Habits and Reaching Your Goals* that there are two ways to categorize them: as mastery or as performance.[2] Mastery-based goals are focused on improving skill and applying consistent effort, while performance-based goals focus solely on achievement.

With a performance goal, Ravey says, failures are tied to a person's belief in their own ability, and setbacks can get in the way of progress. The amount of energy you put into achieving your goal seems wasted if the actual outcome is never reached. It doesn't matter if you've improved your skill or gotten real enjoyment out of the learning process: If you set yourself a performance goal and didn't "perform," that's what you'll focus on.

Mastery goals, on the other hand, encourage consistency. Your focus on learning and development means that setbacks are just a sign you're figuring out what works and what doesn't. Energy used isn't wasted; it's taught you something. By tying your goal to your ability and not one single achievement, you also make it long-lasting and sustainable.[3]

In the case of my own goal, wanting to write a bestselling debut is a performance-based goal, whereas "develop my novel-writing skills" is based in mastery. I can hope that my skills improve to the point that I have a finished manuscript in my hands, but I won't measure the achievement of my goal by any external factor, like its sales figures.

Making the switch from performance to mastery goals is difficult. In her book on how our mindset affects our achievement, American psychologist Dr. Carol Dweck cites author Malcolm Gladwell's suggestion that "as a society we value natural, effortless accomplishment over achievement through effort." It is this, she says, that has partially contributed to the belief that our ability to achieve is fixed within us, that "natural talent" is the sole determining factor of success.[4] This fixed mindset is also enforced (unintentionally) by our parents and teachers during our upbringing. Perhaps, on getting a good score on a test, we were praised for the score rather than all the hard work and energy that went into learning the material. If our grades began to drop, we might've been told we "can't be as smart as previously thought" or even that we should be punished, with our toys or free time taken away until our results improve.

Tying our worth into these performance-based measures of success only teaches us that failure is bad and that the only thing that really matters is outcome, not process. It makes us feel as though any energy we spend is only valuable if it serves a specific goal. I think this is why so many of us put the majority of our energy into our work, where achievements are easily measured and profit-and-loss sheets prove that our efforts weren't wasted. At home, in our relationships and in our health, the outcomes of our energy aren't so tangible. Setting performance goals within these categories can have detrimental effects: putting pressure on new relationships that pushes them to their breaking point, taking cleanliness to the extreme and making the home a place of stress instead of comfort, equating self-worth with numbers on a scale and on the labels of clothes.

If pacing is to be a lifelong consideration of our time and energy, then long-term goals based on learning and development make the spreading out of our energy easier. A performance goal makes it tempting to put all our energy into one thing—if my goal is to be a bestselling author, then I would want to make every effort to achieve that goal. A mastery goal of developing my skills as a writer, on the other hand, puts no time limit or deadline on my efforts. I can choose the pace at which I pursue it. Every step forward is as valuable as the next, regardless of the time or effort in it.

Energy-Generating: Reaching Milestones, Not End Points

Of course, there are times when we have to set performance-based targets, or they're set for us. You might need certain grades to get into your university of choice. You need to create a great résumé to get an interview for the job you really want. You have to save enough money to buy a car or make rent or pay off your credit card bill.

These achievements aren't long-term goals, but milestones on the path to a goal. In pacing, these milestones serve several purposes: They offer a point of rest and reflection, promote reward, renew motivation, and boost our energy toward the goal.

After you've come up with a goal, you should be able to break it down into milestones, or sub-goals. These milestones are particularly important at the start of a new goal because they reduce the uncertainty of the goal and increase motivation.[5] As you know, uncertainty and a lack of motivation both affect the amount of energy we have and the perceived amount of energy needed to complete a task—without clear milestones, we have less energy and yet we need more of it.

Milestones for my goal could be to finish a chapter, then to produce a complete first draft. Later, my milestones would be to find a publisher and make edits and improvements.

You can think of your milestones as energy-generating, in that they help you keep your pace steady as you pursue your goals. They're also a good point at which to reward yourself for your efforts, which is crucial to gaining a better relationship with your own energy levels and seeing spending energy as a positive, not a negative.

Rewards can take many forms and you likely know what would suit you best. I would, however, caution against using rest as a reward. That would be like rewarding yourself by eating the right amount of food each day or letting yourself sleep for seven hours at night. When you treat your basic needs as rewards, you can easily deny yourself good health because you haven't "earned" it.

A milestone is a good point at which to check in on your goal and reflect on how it has affected your pace. When you design your new pace of life in chapter 13, you'll use estimates for the different energy requirements of activities. But we don't always get our estimation right. When you reach one of your set milestones, you might want to reflect on the time and energy you've put in up to this point and adjust your pace as necessary.

I was working on my novel before I began writing *Pace Yourself*. Then, during the COVID-19 pandemic, I began thinking about energy and fatigue, and how my pacing tactics could help those struggling around me. Putting aside my novel felt like the right choice, and I knew that it would remain one of my goals even if I took a few years away from working on it.

You might also ask yourself if the goal is still a priority for you. It's okay if time and experience has changed what you want. The beauty of mastery-based goals is that they can be stopped without any feelings of guilt or regret. You didn't fail: You learned and developed over time and now you want to move on to something else. You're not giving up, either. You're making a decision and you should feel confident that you are the best person to decide what is right for you.

If you've previously associated changing goals with failure or a lack of resilience, it can be hard to alter your way of thinking. You might even believe that feelings of shame serve as a motivator, that giving yourself permission to stop doing something would cause you to lose your drive and slow productivity. That's not the case.[6] You'll be more successful if you talk to yourself with respect and show yourself some compassion and kindness.

Energy-Conscious: Taking Steps toward Your Destination

So, you've got your goal and the milestones that will mark your path toward it. How do you pace your steps without running straight back into a boom-and-bust pattern?

When pacing, you can think of your activities as demanding low, medium, or high amounts of your energy. It's good to think in these terms while you come up with the small steps you can take toward your goal.

When you plan the steps to your milestones, try not to focus on the time it'll take to reach your reward. Giving in to the tendency to rush things can lead you straight back to the roller coaster you were on before. Instead, focus on what you can do with the *energy* you have, not the limited time.

Remember that a low-energy task isn't necessarily a short one, and a high-energy task won't always take up a lot of your time. When you feel tired, it can be tempting to opt for an activity that is quickly completed, a "get-it-over-and-done-with" way of feeling productive while using little energy. But a task that encourages you to use your energy slowly can feel more enjoyable. For example, the daily step of talking to your siblings will help you reach your goal of being more connected to your family. You could dedicate fifteen minutes of your day to texting or calling them, which would take a little mental and emotional energy. Or, you could spend an hour using the same energy to write out a letter. Both activities have their merits and would be enjoyable for different reasons. Of course, if you have very little spare time, the benefit of writing a letter won't outweigh the cost.

> "Focus on what you can do with the *energy*
> you have, not the limited time."

At the end of this chapter, you'll be tasked with thinking of different steps for each of your goals, ideally with varying energy demands. You'll use this in chapter 13 when you design your new pace of life. As with other changes, it's important that you continue to monitor how your new habits affect your energy and fatigue. If you find that an activity is causing you to feel more exhausted than normal, don't push yourself. This is particularly important for people with ME/CFS.

If you have a condition that causes post-exertional malaise, you're likely to be wary of setting goals. Unrealistic expectations could cause you to push yourself too hard, leading to a flare-up in symptoms and being forced to reduce your vital pace even further. Goals that require physical energy are especially difficult to set when you have ME/CFS, where exercise-based treatments have typically worsened patients' overall health.

You do not have to set yourself goals, but if you choose to, make sure that they are broken down into milestones and manageable steps. Make adjustments whenever you need to and don't entertain thoughts of failure or disappointment—you are not your achievements. Your achievements serve you and your experience, not the other way around.

Don't Get Back in the Line

Old habits die hard, and as you design your steps and set your milestones, be wary of getting back in the line for the boom-and-bust roller coaster.

Our levels of energy and fatigue will naturally fluctuate and the demands of life will peak and dip. By now, you should be able to tell the difference between life off and on the roller coaster.

Key to avoiding rejoining the line is to know how you got there in the first place. Take a moment to consider how you've set goals in the past. Have all your goals been your own, or were they influenced by things like fear, others' expectations, and societal notions of what success does or doesn't look like? Did your own wants get lost among thoughts of when you *should* go to university, when you *should* get a promotion, when you *should* settle down and start a family?

These expectations and pressures don't just influence your overall goals: They can determine the daily steps you take, such that you act in ways you think you ought to rather than how you feel. You're told that you're a hard worker, so you take on as much work as possible to live up to this title. You think you have to be the best romantic partner possible, so you try to do everything you can to demonstrate your love, even to the detriment of your own wants.

These impossible standards also apply to potential partners, causing you more problems in the long run. Then, there are the overwhelming pressures on parents—be strict, but not too authoritarian; be kind, but not a pushover; make healthy meals, but don't set rules that give your child eating problems; praise effort, but don't make them fear rest.

These concerns aren't superficial. As a social species, we care very much about how we're perceived and whether we "fit in." We can and do change our opinions and beliefs to align with our peers, as research into social conformity has shown.[7] Caring about what others think is by no means a negative, but people-pleasing and exhausting yourself to avoid disappointment or criticism won't lead to a happy, healthy life.

The trouble is that the further you move away from your roller coaster, the more you forget how detrimental it is to your health and happiness. You might see people celebrating their achievements on social media, glorifying the never-ending grind, suggesting that you should turn every hobby into a side hustle and put every spare moment into self-improvement. You are only seeing the "boom" of their roller coasters. Sometimes, it will feel like you are the only one pacing yourself, while everyone else storms ahead. You won't see their "bust." Their burnout won't be on TikTok; their poor sleep and lack of rest won't make it onto your Instagram feed.

The temptation to exhaust yourself temporarily for some benefit down the road—work hard *now* to have more money *later*—relies on many assumptions about the benefit and about there being a "down the road" in which to enjoy it. The only thing it doesn't assume is that you *will* be exhausted *now*.

Wouldn't it be better to live happily today? To use your energy in ways that you choose and to feel the contented, satisfied fatigue that comes after a day spent however you desire, instead of the awful exhaustion in the lows of the bust?

TASK

Identify the goals—if any—that you want to pursue over the next year. Don't be tempted to set yourself too many: Between three and five is likely to be manageable. Remember that you aren't setting goals that you'll have to spend the rest of your life reaching. You can choose at any point to let go of a goal that no longer aligns with what you want in life or the values that you hold.

Break each goal down into milestones, then come up with the daily or weekly steps you can take to help you reach each milestone. The aim is to make your steps as realistic as possible, but don't worry too much about their feasibility within your schedule at this stage. You'll be able to figure that out later in chapter 13, as you design your new pace of life.

Goal	Milestones	Steps

5 Principles of Pacing Your Goals

1. We need to have goals in life. The pace at which we pursue goals, however, is often determined not by our own wants and needs but by those around us. Sometimes our brains decide on a pace that is much too ambitious, yet we still criticize ourselves when we fail to live up to these unrealistic expectations.

2. When setting goals, it's better to commit to consistency over outcome. You can do this by reframing goals so that they support the long-term dedication of time and effort, not some arbitrary measure of success.

3. Assigning milestones along the route to your goals can help you create momentum, increase motivation, and offer an opportunity to reflect on whether your goals have changed since you first set them. Be wary of setting strict deadlines for your milestones or falling back into a boom-and-bust pattern in your quest to reach the next checkpoint as fast as possible.

4. Deciding in advance the steps you take to reach your goal can help you set your own pace. Make sure these steps are manageable, short- and long-term, but remember you can and should adjust them as you work your way toward new milestones or change your goals.

5. Don't be tempted to rush your goal attainment or let your pace be dictated by factors not of your own choosing. You deserve to spend your energy on what you decide matters and how you see fit, without jeopardizing your health and well-being in the long run.

eleven

The Happiness of Energy

~~~~~~~~~~

MANY, MANY PEOPLE have dedicated their whole lives to studying the question "What is happiness?" from the philosophers of ancient Greece to the neuroscientists and psychologists working today in universities around the world. There are some brilliant books on the subject, which I'll mention in "Further Reading" at the back of this book, and I can't possibly put everything I could say about the relationship between happiness and energy in this one chapter. I hope you'll forgive me, therefore, for the brevity of my attempt to answer the question.

Scientists generally don't use the term "happiness," it being "too loose a term with many meanings."[1] Instead, they'll talk about "subjective well-being" as an indication of a person's happiness with life overall. This includes your day-to-day experiences as well as your overarching satisfaction with life, and both are important for well-being. If you find ways to be happy daily but consider your life to be pointless or depressing, you'll struggle to find the motivation and energy to pursue your goals. If you believe you have all the elements of a happy life—safe shelter, relationships with others, good health, and financial stability—but are miserable day-to-day and find little joy in the things you do, you'll also feel fatigued and unmotivated. In this later scenario, you may also criticize yourself for feeling this way, accusing yourself of being ungrateful for what you do have and undeserving of your accomplishments.

These two principles of happiness—the day-to-day and the long term—are key to successful pacing.

How Happiness Affects Energy

Some people aren't very good at considering happiness for happiness's sake. Some go to great lengths to avoid happiness: The people-pleaser might consider it selfish, the perfectionist of the view that it's unproductive and unworthy of one's energy.

But the impact of happiness is more than fleeting. Happy people have been shown to have better physical health, are more creative, are more productive, and have better (more supportive and deeper) social relationships.[2] These outcomes are determined by studies that mostly reveal a correlation with happiness, rather than a caus-ative relationship—does happiness lead to results, or do results lead to happiness?

We do know that our in-the-moment feelings of happiness will affect our behaviors. How happy we are impacts what we eat and how well we sleep. Low mood and its lethargy goads us to gorge on foods that will provide a small boost of dopamine, so we reach for sugary drinks, snacks, and fast food.[3] Negative ruminating thoughts, depression, and high levels of stress contribute to insomnia and other sleep problems.[4] These relationships are two-way: Sleep qual-ity has a significant effect on mood the following day,[5] and a healthy diet will lead to better mental health.[6]

Happiness is also tied to feelings of motivation, which, as you know by now, affects how much energy you feel you have and how tired you'll feel after exerting energy. Feeling optimistic, which can increase motivation, has been linked with happiness and high self-esteem.[7]

If happiness promotes feelings of energy, then you can invest your energy in pursuing it without feeling like you are wasting your efforts. The activities that bring you happiness are as worthy of your time and energy as those that bring you closer to your goals.

> "Activities that bring you happiness are as worthy of your time and energy as those that bring you closer to your goals."

Pacing Up For Happiness

When it comes to spending our energy above our vital pace, we can often guilt ourselves into pursuing what we think we *ought* to, rather than what we *want* to. The steps you identified in the last chapter are those you've realized you want to take, but you don't have to use every bit of your energy in the pursuit of goals. As happiness is so important to your overall well-being, your new pace of life should allow you time and energy to explore the things that bring you joy, pleasure, and a sense of purpose.

In this chapter, I'll introduce you to six concepts that can bring more happiness into your life. Some of them will resonate with you more than others, but, as with previous chapters, I encourage you to experiment with your activities before deciding which ones will be placed firmly in your new pace of life.

Seeking Purpose and Pleasure

Are you happy with your life? When was the last time you felt happiness?

When psychologists and philosophers consider happiness, they generally talk about two different types: retrospective and introspective. The first of those two questions above taps into your retrospective feelings of happiness—it asks you to remember and evaluate the things you've done or achieved in order to answer "yes" or "no." The latter question asks you to recall the experience of happiness in the moment.

What did you consider when you attempted to answer the question: "Are you happy with your life?" As we've just covered a chapter on goals, you might've thought about the goals you've reached in the past, or how close you are to making the milestones you set for yourself. Your retrospective happiness tends to be connected to your feelings of fulfillment in life.[8]

Neither type of happiness is better: In-the-moment experience is just as important as the later, reflective evaluation of happiness.[9] We need to find our own optimal balance of these two types of happiness, just as the right balance of rest and activity in our days is unique to us.

Before I understood this, I would often reject opportunities for immediate happiness in order to put my energy toward happiness in retrospect. When given a choice between an activity that was fun and joyful and an activity that made me feel pride and achievement after its completion, I would generally pick the latter. My own happiness was out of balance.

In his book *Happiness by Design*, Professor Paul Dolan explains that we need both purpose and pleasure in our life in order to be happy.[10] When deciding how we spend some of our energy, then, we might consider activities that focus on either (or both!) of these feelings.

What gives you purpose? This might be your work or your family. It might be your religion or spiritual practice. It may be tending to your plants, spending time with pets, learning new skills, or sharing memories with loved ones.

Where do you get pleasure? Do you ever make time for play or creativity? When was the last time you felt excited, when your heart pounded, not from stress but from a thrill? Can you afford to sometimes spend money on what brings you joy rather than what is economical?

Viewing your activities through a purposeful or pleasurable lens can sometimes paint the less enjoyable tasks in a happier light, or at least make them more tolerable. If you're at a point in life where all your energy is going to activity that is either mundane or unpleasant—I'm thinking about those weeks spent studying for exams, where each day was just a repetition of the last and each lesson a revision of facts and figures; or perhaps the first experience of parenting, when joy has to be found between endless diapers and sleepless nights—setting aside just a few minutes to consider the purpose in your actions and imagining the long-term benefits of your short-term discomfort can help you feel a little less begrudging.*

Experience or Purchases

I can't tell you how to spend your money, no more than I can say how you should spend your time and energy, but when you consider how to pace for happiness, it's important to think about some of the myths and misunderstandings about the things that do make people happy.

Do money, fame, beauty, and material possessions make people happy? Professor Sonja Lyubomirsky, who has dedicated most of her career to studying human happiness, says that *having* these things is associated with happiness, but *pursuing* them is associated with unhappiness.[11]

While there is a correlation between income and happiness, one major study from 2023 concluded that the link was "weak" and depended on circumstance: If you were happy, more money would likely sustain or improve your positive feelings.[12] But if you were unhappy, an increase in income above $100,000 wouldn't have any impact.

---

* There is a fine line between reframing for happiness and toxic positivity, of course. Thinking "happy thoughts" cannot cure pain or make an unsafe situation acceptable.

Seeing as most of us don't have complete agency over our income—our wages, bills, and living costs being determined largely by external parties—it seems arguably more important to concern ourselves with the things that we *do* have some control over. So, how can our choices lead to more happiness?

Take retail therapy, for example. Can spending money on things make you happier? In the moment, spontaneous purchases can improve mood,[13] but this can, of course, lead to feelings of guilt and regret. Over time, relying on material objects as a source of happiness can lessen the impact of each individual purchase.[14] This is what's known as hedonic adaptation, when each positive feeling needs to be bigger than the last to meet our raised expectations. When our present circumstances change for the better, because we've bought a new house, perhaps, or a new handbag, the initial happiness quickly falls away and becomes part of normal life.

Most of the evidence suggests that spending time, money, and energy on experiences rather than material possessions makes people happy.[15] While the positive feelings incited by a purchase tend to deflate quickly, the happiness we get from an enjoyable activity is said to last longer. Hedonic adaptation is slowed by intentional, novel experience, according to Lyubomirsky.[16] Studies suggest that experiences tend to make people happier than material purchases because we obsess over choosing the best deal, the best quality, the most fashionable, when buying something.[17] But when we choose an experience or activity, we are satisfied with what we can reasonably do. Our need to "maximize" each purchase means we spend a lot of time comparing options, comparing the things we own to the things others have, and ruminating over all the items we could've bought but didn't. We spend a lot of energy thinking, with a low return on happiness. An activity still uses energy, but it has the potential for a much greater impact on our happiness.

It's important to treat your activities as experiences, not "nonmaterial possessions."[18] A good example of this is going to a gig and recording the whole concert on your phone. Why are you doing it?

Because, you say, you want to remember it later. You want to share it with others; you want to watch the recording later and say, "I was there when ..." You want this experience to become one of your non-material possessions.

How often do you watch all the other recordings you've taken? How fleeting is the feeling of twenty likes on your Instagram post? You're forgoing happiness now for some imagined pleasure later—but it will never be as great as experiencing the moment.

I'm not suggesting you stop making any and all purchases outside of your basic necessities. There is joy in treating yourself, in being surrounded by items you've worked hard to pay for. But remember to balance these happy purchases with experiences of real time happiness.

You might also apply this to purchases you make on behalf of others. Would a physical birthday gift bring your partner more happiness than a new experience that both of you can enjoy, not just in the moment but in memory also? Does your teen *need* more shoes, or would they benefit more from a trip out with their friends? It's worth experimenting with experiences as gifts, especially if they spread the happiness across many individuals.

> "It's important to treat your activities as experiences, not 'nonmaterial possessions.'"

Alone or with Others

We need to spend time around other people, specifically people whom we can feel connected to and supported by. When we believe ourselves to be isolated from others, we are lonely, and loneliness has serious, far-reaching impact on our health and well-being. Feelings of loneliness have been linked with depression, poor sleep, a lack of physical and mental energy, and altered immunity.[19]

When we spend time with others, we satisfy certain psychological needs, including a sense of safety, support, and relatedness.[20]

Though we need close bonds, we can also get happiness from strangers by complimenting them or showing kindness, studies have found.[21]

Lyubomirsky recommends making a conscious effort to enact social behaviors in the name of happiness, either by performing kind acts or expressing gratitude for others.[22] It sounds unlikely, but several studies have shown that we're happier when we spend money on others compared to buying something of the same cost for ourselves.[23] Perhaps, if you're tempted toward retail therapy, you might replace it with gifting therapy.

Happiness can come from being with others, but that doesn't mean every social interaction will make you feel happy. Your social needs are likely different from mine, to those of the people around you. But you do need "social nourishment," as Dr. Jeffrey Hall refers to the benefit of interaction. According to Hall, you should think of satisfying your social needs as you do your hunger, your thirst, your fatigue.[24]

You may have heard that extroverts gain energy from social situations, while introverts use energy in them. But this is not the case. Everyone uses energy when they socialize.[25] What's more, our propensity for socializing can't really be categorized as extrovert or introvert—we actually exist on a scale somewhere between the two, with each of us having some extroverted and some introverted qualities. You may fall more toward "extrovert," in which case you'll likely use less energy in social settings than those who are more introverted, *but you'll still use energy.*[26]

When you're living with lower energy, you may think the cost of socializing outweighs the benefits. If we can get happiness in other ways, why spend your limited energy on attending draining social events?

It is important to get "social nourishment," not just from your immediate family or the people you live with, but from friends, colleagues, and strangers. The impact of the COVID-19 pandemic and resulting lockdowns shows that our mental health and well-being are tied to these experiences.

How much energy you spend on socializing in your new pace of life is up to you, but be careful that you're not underestimating the benefits that come from being around others.

If you've neglected your social life for a period of time, you should expect to find social activity more tiring than you remember. According to Hall, people can get accustomed to less or no interaction, so that social activity requires more energy from them when they try to do it. We can develop and build on our social skills, but be patient as you exercise them.[27]

While digital connection is generally not as socially nourishing as in-person communication, according to Hall, technology can provide feelings of love and belonging.[28] A phone call or text exchange could make all the difference to someone feeling totally desperate and isolated, he says. For many, the internet has allowed friendships and connections to flourish across continents—I've managed to find a community of people with ME/CFS who've shown me kindness and support without us ever leaving our homes.

When you feel content with your amount of social contact, whether online or in person, you also gain the ability to find happiness alone. Solitude doesn't feel lonely.

To enjoy your own company involves being happy in what you do and happy in your thoughts. What do you associate with being on your own? Are you able to find happiness in the things you do and think about, or do you ruminate over past mistakes, worry about your situation now and in the future, or otherwise spend your energy in ways that make you unhappy?

At the end of this chapter, you'll make a list of activities you can do that make you happy, including those that you do alone. It's important that you build a good relationship with yourself—you're the person you'll socialize with most often! But, paradoxically, spending time with others can make you feel happier during those periods of solitude. If you never ate enough, you'd feel hungry 24/7: When you eat well, your stomach is satisfied in between meals. In the same way, when our social needs are being met, we are happy to be alone, says Hall.[29]

Putting Happiness into Practice

To bring happiness into your new pace of life, focus on the variety and frequency of your efforts, not on the intensity of feeling. The odd occasion of euphoria among many more periods of low mood isn't likely to make you feel happy day-to-day or long term, but regular, positive feelings can satisfy your retrospective and introspective measurement of happiness.[30]

When you decide to put happiness in your new pace of life, you also commit to noticing your positive feelings in the moment. You might think this planning takes the fun out of happiness, but there's a difference between scheduling and forcing—deciding to do an activity doesn't mean you should put pressure on yourself to be happy no matter the situation around you or your internal feelings. Sometimes, things that you thought would make you happy don't have their desired effect. That's natural. Some activities will require you to be in a certain emotional state or have more energy than you currently do. You know that using physical energy can boost your mood, but if it also causes a flare-up in symptoms or means you can't use your energy on something else you really wanted to do, the net result will not be happiness. It's important to realistically consider the overall impact of an activity. In one study, people who were depressed found that expressing gratitude for others by writing a letter actually induced feelings of guilt.[31] The high emotional energy demand outweighed the benefit of the activity.

When I say *plan for happiness*, I don't mean to imply that your activities, or even your way of thinking about your activities, are the sole determinant of your happiness and life satisfaction. Your genes have an influence on your happiness, as do your life circumstances, though to what extent these things determine the way you feel is not agreed upon by scientists. But your behavior and thinking do play a part,[32] and they're the only things you have any meaningful control over. Have confidence in your own ability to foster happiness in your life. Your influence holds way more power than you think.

Take What You Can

There will, of course, be times in your life when your feelings of joy are sporadic, and you'll have to take what you can get. In these periods, don't let opportunities pass you by. Even the smallest moments of joy can provide energy or reduce the weight of your exhaustion.

When life offers you these opportunities, you might be tempted to avoid them. Prioritizing happiness, even for a few minutes a day or one or two hours on a weeknight, can feel unnatural, possibly selfish, while your to-do list remains full. Spending your money on things that are fun is hard to do when there are basic necessities to buy and bills likely to increase.

You won't be able to *always* choose happiness, but be mindful of neglecting it based on emotion rather than logic. If your parents offer to look after your newborn for a few hours so that you can have some time to yourself, you might be inclined to reject—you'll be anxious while you're away from your child, they'll mess up the napping/feeding routine you worked so hard to establish, people will judge you for wanting some time apart. You will come up with a thousand reasons to say "no," but will you consider the benefits to saying "yes"? When it comes to your own health and your ability to look after another, your happiness (and rest) is much more important than always meeting the impossibly high standards set for you.

TASK

Now's the time to think about some of the happy activities you can put into your new pace of life and list their energy needs as well as life impact. Be realistic about the activities you can bring into your pace: According to Lyubomirsky, in order to work for you they'll need to be enjoyable, feel natural and comfortable, and be chosen at your own will (i.e., not because some author told you to do them).[33]

Draw out a table like the one below. Fill in the activities you could do to support your happiness, then add in the estimated energy need for the activity. For each one, consider the "happiness benefit." My chosen activities are given as examples, but the benefits and energy needs will be individual to you and your circumstances. You'll use this table in chapter 13 when designing your new pace of life.

	Activity	Energy need	Happiness benefit
Pleasurable activities	Taking a hot bath	Low	Low
	Eating at a restaurant	Medium	Medium
Purposeful activities	Volunteering	High	High
	Learning a new skill	Medium	High
Experiences	Attending a workshop	Medium	High
	Going on a hike	High	High
Purchases	Buying craft supplies	Low	Low
	Giving a gift to a friend	Low	Medium
Alone	Reading a good book	Medium	Low
	Exercising	High	Medium
With others	Visiting family	Medium	High
	Seeing a close friend	Medium	High

5 Principles of Pacing for Happiness

1. Happiness is worth spending energy on. It contributes to overall health and well-being, providing you with energy and holding steady in times of fatigue.

2. You need a balance of purpose and pleasure in life, though this doesn't mean equal amounts of both. Experiment with different activities in your quest to find the right balance of the two in your new pace.

3. Sometimes, an experience can bring more happiness than a purchase. Above the things we need, spending money on material items does make us happy, but our feelings of joy are likely to last longer if we spent that same amount on an activity.

4. Being around people who are supportive, caring, and share similar interests can make you happy, but you also need to find ways to feel happy on your own. If you're struggling with social connection, it's likely that any time spent in solitude makes you feel lonely—in this case, prioritizing good relationships is probably more important than trying to get all your happiness from within yourself.

5. Small moments of joy can add up. Aim for a good variety of activities when you're first looking to bring more happiness into your life. Frequency, rather than intensity, of happiness is likely to do you more good in the long run.

twelve

Time and Its Limits

THE PASSAGE OF TIME has its own pace, one that we can't have any real control over. Still, there are plenty of books on the subject of time management and so few that discuss our energy levels. Yet time and energy are like partners: The discussion of one almost inevitably brings up the other. They stand, hand in hand, awaiting instruction. Manipulate one and the other will be affected, but too often it's time we try to change, without consideration for the extra energy demands we place on ourselves.

Looking at your relationship with time can reveal some of your beliefs about energy. If you always see spending time and energy as a negative, you'll make choices based on what saves you the most energy, which isn't pacing's goal. The more you save, the harder it will be to spend, as your body gets used to the amount of energy spent each day. You'll also begin to resent or even fear any task that demands a lot of effort. When fun, new opportunities arise, will you let them pass you by because you're saving your energy for something else?

"Beware the barrenness of a busy life" is a quote often attributed to Socrates, though it's apparently actually from a 1908 Christian journal from the United States[1]—not that it rings any less true by being relatively recent rather than ancient Greek. Busyness, and the pride that has been attached to it, seems to represent an unhealthy relationship with time: that its only purpose is to be used up, rather than appreciated, savored, allowed to pass.

But time isn't really ours to use. What *is* ours is our energy, which we currently use as if it were as constant, as free-flowing as time. By untangling the two, however, we can start to form a better relationship with both of them.

How Time Affects Energy

The way we think, talk about, and treat our time affects our feelings of energy. The pressure of a looming deadline and limited time can power us through the night, while a great expanse of time without activity on vacation can make us feel calm.

Professor Cassie Holmes is a researcher of time and happiness, and in her book *Happier Hour,* she explains that the amount of spare time we have at our discretion—in other words, to be used doing things we want to do, rather than things we have to do, like washing the dishes or driving—can affect how tired we feel.[2] Research does show that when we're time poor, we feel unhappy and exhausted.[3] However, her research also suggests that there's such a thing as too much discretionary time, as large amounts of time without purpose each day leads to lower happiness and well-being in life.[4]

Knowing that happiness also impacts your energy levels, it's clear that your new pace of life should include time (and energy) to spend on yourself. According to Holmes's work, our days should have no less than two hours and no more than five hours of discretionary time. Any less and you'll likely feel stressed, rushed, and like you have no autonomy in your life. More than five hours, though, can jeopardize your feelings of purpose, which, as we've learned, affects your levels of happiness.

For many, having two hours each day to spend at your discretion seems like a far-off fantasy. If you spend your time and energy chasing after children from dawn 'til dusk, you'll be left with very little to use on yourself. Even those whose lifestyles should leave them with a couple hours' discretionary time each day can feel time-poor in today's busy-is-better society. If your work demands your attention outside your salaried 9-to-5, or if in every spare moment you feel you have to be doing something productive, you'll struggle to spend any available discretionary time doing what you want. If you do, you probably feel guilty during and after, reinforcing your belief that time spent purely for the sake of your happiness is a "waste" or less satisfying than "productive" time use.

In her book, Holmes points out that the feelings of happiness and energy associated with discretionary time can come from the perception of having free time, not always the reality. The way you view a task can make the difference. Take walking your child to school, for example. You could hurry them along, focusing only on ticking off "school drop-off" from your to-do list while also thinking about your morning meeting, your bursting email inbox, the deadlines looming. Or, you could focus on your present, your choice to walk rather than drive, the extra time with your child before you both start your separate days. Your mindset doesn't actually change the end result (you have to get them there on time, so it's not really a "discretionary" activity), yet it can change how time-poor, or time-rich, you feel in the moment.

Obviously, some mornings you do have to hurry. A lot of your time use is compulsory, not discretionary. Some activities can't be reframed—no one really likes ironing, do they?

In chapter 9, we looked at the pacing mindset and how a sense of autonomy can affect your feelings of energy. If you feel you have a lack of control over where your time and energy go, you're likely to see all activity as compulsory rather than discretionary. Reminding yourself of your agency, however small the choice or simple the task, will help, little by little, to lessen the energy demands of life.

People with moderate-to-severe ME/CFS can sometimes have such limited energy in a day that the majority of their waking hours is spent resting in bed. It may seem like this is an abundance of discretionary time, but as this time cannot be spent in any other way, I'd argue it's the opposite of discretionary. It's even more important, in that case, that there is time and energy autonomy: Even if your vital pace includes only an hour's worth of activity, it must be your decision to undertake it.

Time Management

Most attempts to control the way you spend your time conveniently ignore your feelings of energy or fatigue. Time management methods are generally aimed at maximizing productivity, as if the limiting factor in our ability to get things done is our organizational skills, not our energy levels. "Get up at 5:00 a.m. and check off half the items on your to-do list before nine o'clock!" some say, like your lack of sleep won't impair the quality of your work; or, "Use AI to schedule every minute of your workday," even though your computer's conception of your energy levels won't be flexible enough to accommodate the impact of arguments at home, for example, or a post-workout slump.

Despite time passing at a fairly regular rate, your feelings of energy ebb and flow. This impacts your efforts to manage your time, because, until now, you've probably assumed your energy expenditure to be constant: If an activity took you an hour on Monday, why wouldn't the same event also take an hour on Friday? I hope, by now, you're able to answer that question.

American scientist Douglas Hofstadter wrote in 1979 that humans' temporal predictions always wildly underestimate the time it actually takes to achieve something. He was referring to estimates that scholars made about the ability of chess-playing computers to beat human opponents, which always seemed to be "within the next ten years" even when a decade had passed since the first prediction.[5] This led to what is now known as Hofstadter's law, which states that it always takes longer than you expect, *even when you take into account Hofstadter's law*. You can probably think of examples of Hofstadter's law at work in your own life.

Could Hofstadter's law be rendered obsolete if we considered the energy needed, rather than time? Is it not that we underestimate time, but that we overestimate the constancy of energy over time?

The misconception that energy is constant leads us to believe we're able to rush things, that a faster pace means we'll get more done. Rush through a meeting so you can get back to work, rush to clear your inbox to make space for more emails, rush through work so you can get through your to-do list, rush home to beat the traffic, rush to cook dinner so you can finally put your feet up for the evening. But does all this rushing accomplish more, or does it just make you feel exhausted? Is the aim of life to "get everything done" or is it to enjoy the process? The truth is, you'll never get everything done. If you did, there'd only be more to do.

> "The misconception that energy is constant leads us to believe we're able to rush things, that a faster pace means we'll get more done."

The Freeing Notion of Limited Energy

In his phenomenal book *Four Thousand Weeks*, author Oliver Burkeman recommends embracing the limits of time in life. He writes: "Most of us invest a lot of energy, one way or another, in trying to avoid fully experiencing the reality in which we find ourselves ... that this life, with all its flaws and inescapable vulnerabilities, its extreme brevity, and our limited influence over how it unfolds, is the only one we'll get a shot at."[6]

His book, subtitled *Time Management for Mortals*, is a refreshing refocus on what matters in life. While we could spend our limited time—four thousand weeks, if you live to age eighty—trying to accrue all that we can and accomplish all that we want, we might actually feel more empowered and fulfilled if we were to step more fully into reality. If we embrace our limits, Burkeman suggests, we can decide and focus on what really matters to us.[7]

I'd go a step further and say that we don't just have to embrace the limits of our time here on Earth, but also the restraints on the energy that we have.

Everyone has limited energy. No one can spend energy without needing to rest. Some people can "outsource" their energy needs by hiring cleaners, nannies, or dog-walkers, and if you can afford to lessen the energetic demands of your life I see no reason why you shouldn't. Your energy is not infinite, and you have a right to use what you do have how you want to.

Of course, there are demands on your time and energy that you have no say in. No one has complete discretion over how they use their days: Even those who have all the money in the world still have to sleep, eat, drink, and use the bathroom when their bodies need them to. But once we've completed our vital pace, the energy that we have left is ours to do with whatever we please.

If you can accept that some of your energy is already accounted for—and it is in more ways than one, as your body reserves some of your daily energy for digesting food[8] and keeping your core body temperature stable,[9] among other things—then you'll feel much more inclined to direct what you do control into the activities that matter most. This might be your goals, your happiness, maintaining your social life, or improving your health. It can be all of the above!

To appreciate that your time and energy is limited doesn't mean you should spend every waking moment considering your energy expenditure, or avoiding activity unless it aligns with some greater plan or worthy pursuit. You can do as much harm by using too little energy as you can by using too much, remember. If you excessively worry about the energy costs of your activity, you'll fall into the mindset of believing there are "right" and "wrong" ways to use your energy. Pile this pressure onto your days and you'll end up feeling guilty in whatever you do, because you could always have done something else.

You might think that it's okay to give up the "unproductive," fun activities you could do temporarily so that you can spend your energy on what has the most financial or career-climbing benefit. Pursue productivity *now* so that you can have fun and pleasure *later*, at some far-off point in time when you'll feel like you've done enough and you can finally relax and have a hobby and friendships . . . Well, I'm afraid to tell you that that day won't come. There will always be more money to make, higher positions to hold. But without the balance of rest with activity, of purpose with pleasure, you'll find that happiness is always a step out of reach.

"Wasted" Time and Energy

If we wish to use our limited time and energy wisely, it follows that there are ways to use them unwisely or ways to waste them. In her book, Holmes refers to wasted time as time spent on an activity that is neither fun nor meaningful.[10] Time and energy spent that serve no purpose or pleasure could have been better spent elsewhere, and so we mourn their loss by calling this a waste. This waste hurts even more than wasted money, likely because we believe we can always accumulate wealth, but we can't get back lost time.[11]

I believe there is more damage done than benefit in thinking this way.

When you decide to worry about wasting energy, you're signing up for two things: pre-energy stress over the decisions you need to make and whether they'll "waste" your energy, and post-energy guilt and frustration when some activities don't live up to your expectations, are retrospectively "unworthy" of your time and energy, or reveal themselves to be more energy-intensive than you'd realized.

Pre-energy stress uses your emotional energy like other forms of stress and anxiety. You can believe that you're weighing up the variables and carefully considering each option, but really, you're doing the very thing you're trying to avoid by worrying about wasted energy. The writer Mark Twain is quoted as saying in 1934: "I am an old man and have known a great many troubles, but most of them never happened."[12]

Post-energy considerations of what's wasted can take on a similar pattern as the retrospective feelings of happiness we talked about in chapter 11. Experiences, according to researchers Kahneman and Riis, are generally categorized, retrospectively, based on what we feel at their end or their most intense moment. This is called the peak-end rule.[13] The peak-end rule suggests that our retrospective evaluations aren't to be wholly trusted: If our feeling at the end or peak of an activity isn't of it being "fun" or "meaningful," we will probably consider it to be a waste of time, even if the overall outcome would indicate that it wasn't wasted. Are there any activities you've done over the last couple of weeks that you consider a waste of your time and energy? Can you identify the peak and end feelings associated with this task? What about the in-the-moment experience?

I appreciate that for people (like me) who experience post-exertional malaise, "wasted" energy comes with a greater cost. If an activity causes a flare-up in symptoms and doesn't bring me any joy or serve a purpose, it's not just time wasted—it has impacts that extend beyond the time spent, affecting how I can act in the following hours and days. Before every activity, then, is a calculation of how this particular use of energy could affect future uses.

Understanding the energy demands of activity helps you pace your days, but if taken to the extreme, it can hold you back from doing the things you really want to do. Your energy estimates—and that's all they can be, because the energy you use is affected by so many uncontrollable variables—will not always be right. Sometimes, you'll overestimate, and find yourself still wired and twitching at bedtime. On other occasions, you'll underestimate. An activity will tire you out much more than you expected. The difference, though, will be that you'll notice this fatigue as it begins, and you'll be equipped to deal with it by resting, returning for a while to your vital pace, and adjusting your energy estimates for that activity in the future.

There's also the possibility of looking back on time and energy spent and seeing them as wasted if you don't do something. For example, when you've spent a year working toward a two-year qualification but have come to realize the course isn't what you want to do after all, or the certificate won't help you much in the future. Yet, because you've already invested both time and energy, you justify spending more of both so as not to write off what you've already used as "wasted."

This is an example of what's known as the *sunk cost fallacy*. It's a mental calculation often taught in economics, that "people will throw good money after bad."[14] We don't like to feel like we've wasted money (or time or energy), so when we're met with an opportunity to either accept a loss or potentially recoup by investing a little extra, we're inclined to take the latter route. But sunk costs should be ignored.[15] They're already sunk; the year you spent learning has already passed. All that staying on would do is enable you to reframe the year and its cost in your mind to make it more palatable.

Instead, when faced with a sunk cost, consider the decision you'd make if no energy had already been used. If someone approached you and said, "Do you want to do a year's course that won't be of use to you?" your response, rationally, should be, "No."

Learning from Your Waste

Consider some of the things you view as "wastes" of time and energy. I'm willing to bet that social media is on your list. As we talked about in chapter 7, social media uses our energy in subtle ways, playing on our emotions and slowly draining our mental energy under the guise of "inactivity."

Why, then, do we spend so much time on social media? And it is a significant amount, the average in 2023 being between two and three-and-a-half hours each day, according to research by GWI, the Global Web Index.[16] That's a lot of energy potentially "wasted."

But if you agree with Holmes that a waste would be an activity that is neither fun nor meaningful, then it's not so much how long you spend on your phone as what you do while you use it. When you use your phone to connect in a positive way with other people, thus promoting feelings of acceptance and belonging, you increase your overall well-being.[17] If your experience online leads to feelings of isolation and lowered self-esteem in comparison to others, it could be doing more harm than good.

While I use my phone to check in on friends, share activities, and speak to those I love, an honest reflection of the time and energy I spend on social media reveals that I mostly engage with content that depicts a life I want to lead. My social platforms show me famous writers, chefs, scientists, all sharing their curated lifestyles. I like to think I'm viewing their content to learn from them, and sometimes I do pick up a good recipe or new research paper, but when I put my phone down, I find myself comparing my life to theirs, wishing mine were different.

Yet the next time I'm sitting in front of the computer, struggling to think of what to write next, I'll still feel the urge to pick up my phone and scroll. Even though I know it won't help me write, nor will it make me feel better about my writer's block, I'm tempted.

Like me, you may use social media as a distraction from other, more energy-demanding activity. You might've noticed that the reward you feel when you pick up your phone is minimal, but preferable to the discomfort of sitting with your difficulty. It's easier, requires less effort overall, to scroll through Instagram and watch TikTok videos than it is to strain over your next university assignment or write your weekly team report. Of course, the assignment still needs writing, your report still needs collating, only now you have less time and energy to do it. You could even say you're booming and busting with your procrastination.

Instead of feeling guilty about your "waste," it's better to try to learn why you spent your time and energy in that way. What is it about the task at hand that makes you want to procrastinate? What emotions have you tied to the experience of hard work, so that any task that requires a lot of effort immediately becomes unpleasant and demotivating?

It might be that deep down you believe things that are "right" for you should be effortless. That if you are good at something, it should come easily. If it's hard, it means you're not good enough, and if you're not good enough now, why try to get better? There are plenty of things that you can do that do come easily, so why waste time and energy doing what's hard?

See how, with a certain mindset, doing something difficult can also be considered "wasting time and energy"? Unfortunately, when you're stuck between a rock (the task you don't want to do) and a hard place (the guilt and "waste" of going on your phone), the only way out is to make a tough decision. An hour from now, where do you want to be: sitting atop the rock looking at how far you've come, or at its base, looking at what you still have to climb?

> "Instead of feeling guilty about your 'waste,'
> it's better to try to learn why you spent your
> time and energy in that way."

5 Principles of Time and Energy

1. Discretionary time is the number of hours you have each day to spend doing what you want, not what you're obligated to do. Having too much or too little discretionary time has negative effects on your feelings of energy and fatigue.

2. Though it's tempting to rush through tasks to get more done, you need to acknowledge that there is a limit to your daily energy expenditure. Rushing won't give you more energy to spend: It'll tire you out faster.

3. If you constantly consider whether your time and energy are "wasted," you'll exert much more energy in the long run as you stress over each activity and anxiously debate with yourself over the smallest of decisions. Though pacing invites us to choose which activities use our energy, taken to the extreme this thinking can make you avoid energy expenditure altogether—making you more fatigued in the long run.

4. Beware the sunk cost fallacy. Time and energy spent are gone; there's no bringing them back. Don't feel like you have to continue with an activity, a goal, a relationship, just because you've "invested" in it thus far.

5. When you notice yourself feeling frustrated at a lack of time or of energy wasted, take the opportunity to learn about your own beliefs. Why do you feel like time has to be spent in a certain way? What stops you from deciding how best to spend your time and energy?

thirteen

Design

~~~~~~~~

The Ten Steps to a
New Pace of Life

NOW IT'S TIME to put what you've learned into practice, to craft a schedule that sets a better, more balanced pace of life in which you can reach your goals, be happy, and spend your energy the way you want.

This schedule will build upon the vital pace that you set in chapter 8, and the focus will be on the energy that you use throughout your weeks rather than the activities themselves. Over time, you'll notice that the things you do will take less energy than they once did, so you can increase their length or intensity or add in new activities in what we call "pacing up." I recommend reflecting on your schedule every two to four weeks, adding in new activities or adjusting your balance of activity and rest when you feel ready. This isn't an equation for adding ever more and more to your schedule, though. You are not a machine whose productivity should be increased, updated, or improved to always perform better and better. You can find the pace that suits you and stick to it, without guilt or frustration.

The goal isn't to create a rigid, minute-by-minute schedule that you must follow at all times. As mentioned in chapter 9, you also need freedom and flexibility in your new pace of life. Trust that you now know how best to spend your energy.

Step 1: Choose Your Starting Ground

I prefer to design my schedule on paper and in pencil first so that I can make changes as I go. But if you'd like to use an app or desktop calendar, or any kind of physical diary, that's fine, too. What matters is that you set down your design somewhere so that you can refer back whenever it seems your energy is being used in a way you hadn't intended.

My weeks tend to follow the same pattern, so I usually stick to planning seven days at a time. If you work on a rotational schedule, or have different commitments week to week, you might find it easier to design a month or even a single "working day" and a "nonworking day."

Step 2: Outline Your Set Times

Some of the activities in your vital pace will be bound to a certain time—taking the kids to school, attending a course or class, joining a weekly meeting. Put these in your schedule by outlining the time they occur. Leave space for notes or edits, as you'll further divide these activities up in a moment.

If you have set times for anything else, whether that requires physically being somewhere or just completing activities within a certain period, go ahead and outline these in your schedule, too. If you have to work 9-to-5, outline this time, knowing that this period will be divided up into individual tasks and activities in a moment. Anything that can't occur at any other time of day should be outlined at this point, including your commute, mealtimes, and your sleep.

Step 3: Put in Your Vital Pace

Using the remaining activities you identified as being part of your vital pace, begin boxing out more time in your schedule. If an activity falls within one of the set times you created in Step 2, create a smaller box within the set period.

When placing these activities, think about the energy that they'll use. Remember that some people feel more creative in the morning, while others feel more analytical. If your pacing diary revealed that some important tasks routinely made you feel tired, consider placing them at a different time of day. You'll be able to tweak and amend your pace going forward, so feel free to experiment with your time and energy.

Once you've placed your vital pace, note the type of energy that these activities will use. I like to assign a color to each type: blue for emotional, red for mental, green for physical. If you're using an app or digital calendar, you can usually adjust the color or design of entries.

I draw a thick outline around my activity to make it obvious which energy I'll be needing. Of course, some activities will use more than one type, but usually there is one that'll be drained more than others. Sitting at my desk working does take some physical energy—I fidget, sometimes stand, stretch my arms, and so on—but it's mainly mental work, so it's outlined in red.

At this point, you might notice there is an imbalance in the energy you use across the day or week. That's okay. As most of the activities you've placed so far will probably be work-related, the nature of your work will dictate the energy already allocated. My schedule, in this step, shows a lot of red and not much else.

Step 4: Add in Time to Spend Energy on Your Goals

Now, place in the steps you identified in chapter 10 as helping you reach your milestones. You'll need to estimate roughly how long you might need to spend on these steps, which you know isn't easy to do, given Hofstadter's law that things always take longer than expected.

You may need to come back and edit these times after the first few weeks.

Think about the energy demands of these steps when you decide where to place them. If the activity uses mental energy and is not work-related, you might want to place it on a weekend. Don't cram too much into any one day, or you'll end up planning another boom-and-bust life. In Step 6, you'll place some rest activities in your schedule, which may involve moving around some of the activities you've put in at this stage. Color these activities depending on their main energy type.

Step 5: Put in Your Happy Activities

Knowing how important your happiness is to your energy levels, well-being, and health, it's key that you commit time and energy to doing what makes you feel good. You can place a few of the specific activities you identified in chapter 11; however, you may just want to set aside an hour or an evening for happiness, letting whatever feels good at the time dictate the activity. Variety is good for happiness.

You could schedule some "physical happiness" on an evening when you know you'll have a tough work-from-home day, which you can use to exercise, explore your local village or park, or spend with your partner. Or, on a weekend, you might want to invest some energy in an activity that uses your mind, like trying a new hobby or taking a class that involves learning a new skill. Again, outline these activities in the color or design that corresponds with their main energy. Remember to set aside time and energy for socializing. You don't have to use these slots for physical meetups: You could call your parents, send voicemails to friends who haven't heard from you in a while, or just catch up on unread texts. You can schedule this time as often or infrequently as you like, but I think it is worth doing, especially if you're the kind of person who uses their phone to procrastinate.

Given that purposeful activities can make you feel happy, it's good to indicate any tasks in your vital pace that might also bring you some joy. I suggest making these feelings obvious by thinking about them during the activity, which you might do by scheduling a "two-minute check-in" in your diary, or setting a reminder on your phone with the prompt: "Write a sentence about what's made you feel a sense of purpose today." It may seem like analyzing these activities could reduce their impact on your happiness, but studies do suggest that people who regularly reflect on the day's events and focus on what they are grateful for actually feel happier in life.

> "Knowing how important your happiness is to your energy levels, well-being, and health, it's key that you commit time and energy to doing what makes you feel good."

Step 6: Make Time for Rest

Take a moment to assess the activities you've placed in your schedule. Are there any that could be considered restful? Is there any type of energy you use a lot of, but currently have little time to recoup?

Always err on the side of giving yourself more rest than you need, especially if you have a condition that causes fatigue or limits your energy. As you'll be reassessing your schedule, you can always remove or shorten some restful activities, but if you don't plan enough at the beginning you could worsen symptoms and risk booming and busting again.

Slot in some of the activities from your Rest Bank throughout your day. Don't assume that rest should always come *after* activity. You may find that certain types of rest are better had before or during energy expenditure—I schedule emotional rest before social events and plan for five to ten minutes of mental rest after every sixty to ninety minutes of mental activity. This is especially important for work meetings, where I'm using both types of energy!

Step 7: Schedule the "Meh" Stuff

There's no getting around the fact that we all have to use our energy in ways we don't want to. Chores and life admin demand time and energy, though we might choose to ignore them and end up paying the price: living in conditions that make us miserable, missing important deadlines, and always playing catch-up.

You might, conversely, be spending too much time on these things currently compared to the people around you or because you or others are holding you to unreasonably high standards. In some shared spaces, women bear much more of the weight of housework. Working mothers are said to spend five hours (!) more on chores each week than working fathers.[1]

First, there's a conversation to be had about the amount of time and energy needed to complete your housework and other "meh" tasks. I'd recommend repeating the task at the end of chapter 11, in which you calculated the happiness benefit and energy cost of some activities. This time, list your "meh" activities and assign them values of high, medium, and low priority. Then, decide whether you want to focus just on the high tasks for the first iteration of your new pace (which I'd recommend) or, if you really feel it's necessary, choose to prioritize both the high and medium tasks. Remember to set your own standards for what's needed. You don't have to live in a home that looks like it belongs in a glossy magazine, nor do your kids always have to wear perfectly ironed T-shirts or eat off an immaculately laid table. If your energy is better placed elsewhere, you're allowed to compromise here.

If you are able to share these tasks with others, like housemates or family, I suggest having a deliberate discussion about how things are distributed. There's an argument for assigning tasks based on who finds them easier, or who dislikes them the least, but generally the sharing of all chores is likely to make everyone happier.[2] This may seem surprising—wouldn't it be better for one person to do all the washing up, another to always do the vacuuming, and so on?

Consider a home where one partner gets the more "fun" jobs, like cooking and tending to houseplants, while the other washes the dishes and cleans the bathroom. These are four physical tasks that seem to be divided fairly, yet one partner will see rewards at the end of their chores—a nice plate of food, the blossoming of roses—and another will simply see shiny ceramic waiting to get dirty again. With a more equal distribution (both parties do all four tasks, half the time), there's less chance of the "grass is greener" effect, and each person can appreciate the differing energy consumption and rewards. It won't work for everyone, but it's certainly worth trialing for a few weeks.

In terms of scheduling time for chores, sorting out bills, or general life admin, there are two options: Spread them out over the week and do a small amount daily, or block out one or two chunks of time each week to get the "meh" out of the way. I find that low-energy tasks are better completed little and often, while high-energy tasks should be consolidated. Both options have pros and cons:

- **Little and often.** Going by what we discussed in chapter 9, the best way to form habits is to make the behavior small and low in effort. So, if you need to get better at completing a chore or opening your mail, it's good to make the activity short and sweet. Doing this every day can anchor your behavior in routine, which lowers the amount of motivation you actually need to implement the behavior. I use this tactic to do the washing up: Every morning, after I drink my first cup of coffee (my prompt), I do the washing up. There's usually only yesterday's mess to clear, as I'd done the task yesterday morning, so the task is relatively low effort compared to letting the dishes pile up for a few days. Of course, I follow this habit with a reward: my second cup of coffee. However, if you really, really dislike the task, by spreading it out across your week you're just adding a little bit of unhappiness to every single day. You may instead want to consolidate your chore into one, longer session, and employ another tactic to make it less "meh."

- **Everything all at once.** Some tasks need more time and energy, but that can make them boring or frustrating, as you might feel you could be doing something "better." The best way I've found to combat this is to combine these activities with something that is fun or purposeful. Listen to a podcast or an audiobook while you clean, fold clothes in front of the TV, use your bills and letters to make origami (once you've finished with them, obviously). Remember the peak-end rule from the last chapter? We tend to categorize memories as good or bad based on what happens either at the end of the event or at its most intense moment. Knowing this, can you alter your activities so that you end on a happier note? This won't always work and maybe you'll never look forward to an evening of cleaning, but at least some of the frustration, and emotional energy, attached to your task might be lessened.

Step 8: Protect Spare Time and Energy

At this point, you'll have a good design for your new pace of life. If you feel like you have spare time and energy, you can plan in a few more activities, but I do think it's best to only add more after a few weeks at a certain pace.

There are temptations to spend whatever you have spare, though. A new project at work, a favor asked by a friend, a voluntary position in an organization you care about. In these instances, you may want to immediately say yes and find a way to fit them into your new pace of life, but it's worth stopping to think about their overall impact, and what you'll have to reduce or stop in order to undertake them. It's tempting to remove a restful activity, or a step toward one of your goals, but this may upset the balance of activity across your week. If you do want to fit it in, make sure you return to your schedule and figure out how you can do so without falling back into a boom-and-bust pattern of energy use.

When someone asks me to do something, or offers me any new opportunity, I always employ a "double it" rule. Given Hofstadter's law, that everything takes more time (and energy) than we expect, I imagine that whatever is being asked of me is actually doubled. My friend wants me to help her study one night a week; what would be the impact on my overall pace if I had to spend two nights' worth of energy? If a new employee network is looking for helpers for two hours every Wednesday, could I afford to give them four hours' worth? If the answer is still yes, then I find a way to fit it into my schedule. If not—if there are too many valuable things needing that time and energy—I let the opportunity go to someone else.

There are times when energy shared is energy halved, but it's important to know when this does and doesn't apply. Cooking with a friend or partner can make the activity less energy intensive (you're not responsible for all the mental energy of preparing the meal, nor the physical energy) and is a fun, happy way to spend some time. But when entire teams dedicate an hour of their day to a meeting that could've been written up and disseminated in two hours (or less!) by the host, the overall result is more energy used.

Step 9: Make Some Rules

In Part Two you identified some of the ways you could improve your diet and sleep to reduce your feelings of fatigue. Knowing what you do now about habits, are there any rules you can create about how and when you'll make these changes? If you decided to take a "free trial" of better hydration, can you find a behavior and prompt that'll help you drink more water? Are there any habits you can create that will give you better sleep hygiene—winding down without technology, making your bedroom a place for sleep only, limiting alcohol consumption, and so on?

If you've identified social media as an unnecessary drain on your energy, or as a procrastination tool, you might want to trial a rule about how and when you use these sites. Maybe you say you won't use your mental energy on your phone when you want to put it toward work. Perhaps you want to prioritize connecting with your partner or family in the evening, instead of strangers online.

In making these rules, which are essentially about breaking habits, you generally need to make the behavior as difficult as possible to perform. Don't rely on willpower to stop you taking your phone out of your pocket or opening up Facebook in your browser: Put your phone in another room and find a way to block social media sites on your laptop during work hours. If you need your phone for work, or use social media as part of your job, find ways to limit other use during these times—don't have your personal account logged in, or schedule "work phone time" so that you know when your phone should be with you and when it can be far away. In essence, you're setting a rule and taking away the ability to break it.

Invite others into your rule-setting so that they can see the thought process behind any new boundaries you've set that will affect them. These conversations may reveal some surprising consequences that would've been a problem if they'd been left to fester: Your friend might explain her anxiety around your reduced contact, or your partner may express their concern that you'll want to change their habits as well as your own. You're not expected to be able to guess these impacts in advance, but giving the people in your life the opportunity to speak will help you protect your relationships in your new pace.

You'll need to decide which boundaries are flexible, which rules can be bent, and where to draw the line. As with all your other new habits, remember that you can always end a "free trial" or take on something new just to see how it fits within your complicated life. Pacing is largely about finding what works for you and your energy levels. You don't have to get it right the first time.

"You'll need to decide which boundaries are
flexible, which rules can be bent, and where to
draw the line."

Step 10: Assess Your Balance

Some days will look busier than others, sometimes you'll have to use more of one type of energy than another, but overall, your new pace of life should avoid the big booms and terrible busts of your previous way of living. You shouldn't have all your activity during the week, with resting reserved for weekends. You should have ways to be happy scattered across your schedule so that you're not simply living through Monday to Friday just to have fun one or two nights a week.

Eventually, some of the activities you do will take less energy than they did at the start. As you get used to doing more, whether that's mental activity or exercise or socializing, you'll find it easier to pace up and add new activities to your schedule. If, at any point, things start to feel like too much, you can return to your vital pace or go through this chapter again to bring your life back to the pace you designed.

I hope this exercise of scheduling your time and energy helps you feel like you have more control over your life than before. Yes, there are things you have to do, but you can find ways to enjoy doing them, or at least lessen their negative impact on your overall energy, health, and happiness.

Conclusion

~~~~~~~~~~~~~~~~~

Pacing for Life

Where pacing differs from other life-hacking techniques or time management attempts is that it's not about productivity. It's not a method for performing your best or achieving everything you can within your field. It's a lifestyle, one that should be as flexible as life itself—as surprising and enjoyable and sometimes challenging.

I am wary of suggesting that pacing is a way of finding work/life balance, mainly because I absolutely hate the phrase "work/life balance." It implies that "work" is separate from life yet holds an equal standing. If you believe that "life" is everything that isn't work, then do the hours you spend working put life on hold?

No, life goes on; we find out personal news during work hours, we see children pop up in Zoom meetings, and we turn to colleagues for advice and support about all manner of things unrelated to the job.

Work isn't confined to the hours we spend working, either. It's what we think about when we plan for the future, working out whether we can afford to live in a new house on our salaries or take time off to go on the vacation of a lifetime. Work serves as part of the feelings of purpose we need for happiness, as we discussed in chapter 11.

When people say, "I don't have a very good work/life balance," they often mean, "All my energy goes into my work and I leave nothing left for everything else." While their work booms, the other areas of their life are in bust. It's a pace of life that is unsustainable. I hope that *Pace Yourself* has shown you that there is another way.

Your energy is yours to use and enjoy. There is a value in wisely using what you have, even if much of it has to go on working or taking care of another, even if you have very little to begin with due to ME/CFS or long COVID or any other cause of fatigue.

There is so much in life that you have no control over. As I see it, there are three ways to respond to this fact: by denying it and attempting to live as if you do have control over everything; by acknowledging it and also surrendering what little control you do have; or by appreciating it and enacting control in the small ways that you can.

Denial leads you to believe that if you just play your cards right, you'll be able to do everything you want with your life. That if you try hard enough and become the ultimate productivity ninja, you'll reach a point where you can look back and say, "Aha! Now I'm done with work and I can focus on enjoying life." These people might also say that they look forward to their retirement, because the only way they can conceive of living well is to remove the temptation to work from the equation entirely. Unfortunately, the jobs will never be done, you'll never do it all, and you certainly won't find it easy to switch from a life of high intensity to one of relaxation. That is a boom-and-bust pattern on a very large timescale.

You might respond by conceding all of your control, since so much of it has been taken from you anyway. I certainly felt that way when I had my relapse. Overnight, my energy had been stolen. When I woke up, all I had in me was a vital pace that covered a measly hour and a half of activity. It felt like I'd been the victim of a cruel joke—what was worth doing for just ninety minutes? It was almost worse to have been left with such a little amount than to have woken up with nothing. Even though I'd successfully paced myself before, I couldn't see myself ever having energy again. It was one of the hardest periods I've ever had to live through.

I don't know when I stopped rejecting the control I had and became someone who could find value in the small things under my own influence, but I know I wouldn't have arrived there without everything I'd learned about pacing.

I kept a pacing diary for a long time after my relapse. After a while, I noticed that I felt like I had a bit of spare energy outside my vital pace, so I tentatively added in a new, low-energy activity. I'd increased my total activity to about one hour and forty-five minutes. A couple of weeks later, I felt ready to do the same. I reached two hours a day. About six months after my relapse, I was working a few hours each day and using more energy going for short walks or pursuing hobbies. Now, just over two years later, I've been able to work full-time to write this book. I'm still pacing myself.

"Your energy is yours to use and enjoy."

Pacing in Practice

Pacing, essentially, requires three things:

- An awareness of your own feelings of energy and of the activities demanding too much of you
- A healthy lifestyle to support your energy levels
- An understanding of how you want to use your energy and a commitment to your new pace of life

• • •

There are so many factors that affect your energy levels that it's easier to group them into the categories of emotional, mental, and physical, but of course the lines between these types are much blurrier than they appear here. In knowing how your energy is used and replenished, you're able to respond appropriately when life throws you a new demand or a decision to be made. You can allow things that use your energy to enter your life because you know how to save energy elsewhere, or you can say "no, thank you" with confidence because you realize it would take too much and leave too little.

You also know now how important your diet, sleep, and rest habits are for your energy levels. These things, which are so easily overlooked when you're stressed and burned out, can make such a big difference.

Identifying how and why you want to use your energy isn't always easy, but it's what separates the pace you set for yourself from the one that is decided for you, whether by your brain, your parents, society, or any number of sources. It's how you go from a boom-and-bust lifestyle to one of happiness, health, and energy.

Life

Except, it's not always happiness, health, and energy. Things will happen that upset your pace. You will grieve for lost loved ones, for relationships ending or opportunities taken away. You will experience times of immense pressure, moments of pure joy and elation, and all the while your energy levels will be up and down with you. I don't for a minute think you'll turn back to *Pace Yourself* and spend the time calculating your vital pace or taking out free trials of new sleeping habits. All I can hope is that something you've learned will help soften the blows and lengthen the highs. That when you're ready, you'll have what you need to pull yourself out of the boom-and-bust cycle to return to a steadier pace of life.

Writing this book has been a test of my own ability to pace myself. I haven't always succeeded, and I've had to reduce the energy I put into other goals and happy activities to make these words appear on this page. I've also had to rely on the people around me—without their help in reducing the energy costs of living, I would've struggled a lot more to manage my pace of writing. My husband took on a lot of housework; my parents and in-laws visited to help with cleaning and gave their energy willingly in place of mine. My friends understood that I just wouldn't have the emotional energy to see them or even speak to them as much as I had done previously. When I started writing, my husband and I sat down to talk about managing expectations and compromising on standards. As books and research papers spread about our living room over the following months, we both worked to accept the temporary clutter rather than use emotional energy fighting over it.

I do also know that I would've done a lot of damage to my health and energy levels if I hadn't understood the importance of rest, the depletion of my mental energy, and the ability to form habits that stick.

Designing your new pace of life, as you did in chapter 13, doesn't mean your life will always proceed at one pace. I don't believe that committing your schedule to paper will manifest good energy and dispel exhaustion. As Oliver Burkeman writes in *Four Thousand Weeks*, "We treat our plans as though they are a lasso, thrown from the present around the future, in order to bring it under our command. But all a plan is . . . is a present-moment statement of intent."[3]

Yet making that statement over and over helps you make decisions now and in the future that are good for your own energy. It reminds your brain that it no longer needs to use its ability of teleo-anticipation to pace you toward your goals, because you're quite capable of doing that for yourself.

The Ultimate *Telos*

Aristotle is said to have defined humans' ultimate *telos* as happiness from individual flourishing. He believed that we should intend to be virtuous and show this in our daily actions—it isn't enough to *want* to live in a particular way; we actually have to *live* it.

Perhaps you think you'll pace yourself later, once the busyness of your life has quieted down. Maybe you have one last goal to achieve that absolutely requires you to boom and then bust, then after that you'll be able to try pacing. When the demands on you are less great, when things are more calm, that's when you can afford to manage your energy.

We always think that future-us will have an easier time of it. That we'll be less busy in the future. But it isn't true. Life will always find a way to take up all your energy, and you have to be able to resist it. Everything you want to do will always tempt you, but you can say, "Wait, I'll get to you at my own pace."

This isn't to say that you shouldn't pursue the things that inspire action in you. We need people to petition for better policies, to fight against climate change, to break down stereotypes, protect the rights of others. Why should you care about the balance of your own energy and fatigue, you may ask, when there is so much that rightfully demands your attention?

If we are to have any hope of using our energy to tackle some of the matters we find most pressing, we need to establish a good relationship with our energy levels. A life with purpose is not the opposite of a life well paced. You can do great work and take great care of yourself.

Are You Alive?

There are apparently two types of regrets: those born from action and those from inaction.[1] When you regret doing something, you feel it in the moment—"I wish I hadn't said that," or "I shouldn't have done what I did." These regrets, though real and often heartbreaking, don't tend to linger. They're usually resolved by apologizing or acting to rectify whatever mistake you made.

A regret of inaction, though, tends to stay with us longer.[2] When you miss out on an opportunity or let something pass you by, there generally isn't a way to bring the chance back a second time. These unresolved issues can haunt us. You probably won't look back on your deathbed and regret telling your coworker you fancied her, but you might wish you'd chased after that love you lost because you were too scared to commit or too proud to say sorry.

You can continue to put off thinking about your pace of life, choosing to spend your energy now and worry about the consequences later, but I think that this decision inspires both types of regret. Eventually, you'll burn out and regret the actions that led you to exhaustion. But you'll also regret not acting sooner, not valuing your own energy and your overall health and well-being enough to stop the boom-and-bust pace you've lived by.

The writer Alan Watts has been quoted as saying that people are "like donkeys running after carrots that are hanging in front of their faces from sticks attached to their own collars. They are never here. They never get there. They are never alive."[3]

You can keep running to get there, wherever it is you think you'll reach, and finally feel like you've won at life. Or you can stop, find a steady pace, and feel really alive.

Appendices

~~~~~~~~~~~~

Frequently Asked Questions

Among the ME/CFS community, it's a bit of a running joke that so often you are told to "just learn to pace yourself." It's usually meant well, but rarely followed by "and here's how you *actually* pace." Many people have, then, been left to figure it all out on their own, making mistakes and causing a flare-up in symptoms or, in some cases, increasing the overall severity of their condition.

I've tried to provide here a full, but I hope not overwhelming, framework for pacing. Still, I know there will be some questions about the practicality of pacing and how you might solve some common problems. This FAQ should help, but if you do have any specific queries about pacing, please do get in touch with me via my website, amyarthur.co.uk, where I'll also post any updates to the FAQs page.

I'll also be updating a list of pacing FAQs regularly on my website: amyarthur.co.uk.

How Do I Decide What Should Be Included in My Vital Pace?

Getting your vital pace (chapter 8) right is crucial, but I appreciate that it is also one of the most difficult parts of pacing! It may take a while for you to find the right balance of activity and rest, so don't give up if your first attempt is too intense or too light.

Generally, I'd say it's better to err on the side of including too little in your vital pace than too much, especially if you have a condition that is made worse by overexertion or excess stress.

When considering whether an activity belongs in your vital pace, you might try asking yourself the following questions:

- Does this activity satisfy a biological or physiological need for myself or someone dependent on me?
- Will my income or financial security be directly threatened if I don't do this activity for the next two weeks?
- Can this activity be postponed until I am ready to pace up, or does it absolutely have to occur within my vital pace?
- Is there a way I can lessen the energy demands of this activity? (See chapter 8 for suggestions of how you might do this.)
- Can I effectively delegate this activity to someone else and put it out of my mind so that it doesn't continue using up my energy?
- Am I considering including this activity in my vital pace just because I am worried about what people will say or think if I don't do it for the next couple of weeks?

Your vital pace should be an opportunity for your mind and body to rest. Think of it a bit like a "battery-saving mode," where only the most essential activities are allowed to use your energy.

Remember that adjusting your standards and setting boundaries is as important as choosing the right activities to prioritize. It's likely that your high standards and productivity-over-rest attitude contributed to your boom-and-bust lifestyle and feelings of fatigue. If you really want to set yourself a new pace of life, you'll need to first let go of your unrealistic expectations for your own energy.

When Can I Start "Pacing Up"?

Everyone's pacing timeline is different, so I'm afraid there is no strict schedule I can give you. You might feel ready to do more after just two weeks of your vital pace, or it may be months before you're able to add in even one extra activity. The key will be noticing that the activities in your vital pace are becoming easier and less energy-intensive. You might find that, at the end of the day, you feel you still have energy left to use. If this happens every day for a week or more, then you can try pacing up.

Don't be tempted to add in lots more activity in one go, or you'll put yourself straight back on the boom-and-bust roller coaster. Pacing up is a steady, gradual process that should be enjoyable and rewarding, not pressurized and stressful. There is no deadline, no "perfect pace" to compare yourself to.

Some people rush to pace up because they find their vital pace uncomfortable. It's natural to feel this way, though, after running through life at top speed for as long as you can remember. One of the things your vital pace offers is a chance to reevaluate your beliefs about productivity and success, so that when you do begin pacing up, you don't fall back into a boom-and-bust pattern.

You might, on the other hand, feel reluctant to pace up. This is also common, especially if you have a condition with symptoms that fluctuate. Remember that you can always return to your vital pace if you feel like you are losing control over your energy levels or have taken on too much, too soon. There is no shame in taking a step back now so that you can move forward at your own pace later.

How Do I Explain to My Friends/Family/Colleagues That I Am Pacing?

Pacing affects the people around you in the same way that others' actions and needs affect your energy levels. It's important that you have conversations about your new pace of life and the impact it may have on your relationships.

I would start by explaining why you are pacing. What has led you to reconsider how you use your energy? The people closest to you might know that you've been feeling exhausted, but do they understand why? Try not to assign blame when explaining the boom-and-bust of your previous lifestyle—what matters isn't that your boss always demanded too much of your mental energy or that one of your friends is emotionally draining, it's that you have set yourself new boundaries that mean you'll be more deliberate about your energy use. This, of course, might mean that your boss will have to get used to it when you firmly but reasonably decline to regularly stay later than your set hours, or that your friend will find some conversations paused before they get too exhausting. Explaining why you've set these new boundaries will help others accept them.

You'll also want to explain the benefits of your new lifestyle to your existing relationships. Your new understanding of cognitive effort means you'll be able to work more efficiently and, because you're less fatigued, you'll perform better within your working hours. You'll also be able to better empathize with your friend, knowing that if a conversation about your friend's own life and problems uses *your* emotional energy, it's likely to be draining a lot of your friend's energy, too.

Finally, remind them of what *hasn't* changed. Tell your colleagues that you still enjoy the work you do together and that you value their support. Explain to your family that you love them, and any changes to the amount of energy you put into certain activities are out of respect for yourself, not disrespect toward them. Humans have a tendency to avoid or reject change, especially if there is a lot of uncertainty around the reason for the change or concerns about its validity. Knowing this, try to be as open as you can about the reasons for your new pace of life.

The conversation may turn to their feelings of fatigue or energy. If they think that to rest is to waste time, or that the only worthwhile use of energy is an activity that generates income or leads to "success," they'll find it difficult to align your new pace of life with their beliefs. It may be that they're struggling with feelings of exhaustion themselves but have the mindset that you should just "push through it." If you feel you have the energy, you could try to help them see how it's possible to lead a more balanced life, but know that you're under no obligation to do so.

I Find Resting Frustrating. How Can I Find Ways to Rest That Are Enjoyable?

There are so many different ways to rest that there are bound to be some activities you'll find enjoyable. But I think it's important to ask yourself: Why do I find rest frustrating?

Do you still believe that you should spend as much time as possible being productive? And do you still consider rest to be unproductive? In that case, you'll feel very much like any time spent resting is wasteful, possibly even lazy. But I urge you to think of rest in a different way. As food and drink and sleep provide you with energy, so does rest. Do you consider your mealtimes unproductive, so much so that you avoid eating until you're forced to? Is sleeping so unproductive that you refuse to go to bed until you're falling asleep at your desk? No. Nor should you postpone rest until you are burned out.

It might be that resting makes you anxious because you feel like your never-ending to-do list is simply growing in the background, waiting for you. The stress of the piling demands is likely seeping into your resting mind, making you worry and using up emotional energy. If this is the case, your attempts to rest are unlikely to feel restful at all. There are a few different ways I try to tackle this problem—which I still do face, from time to time! You might try finding a restful activity that occupies your mind, like an engaging TV show or a crossword puzzle. I find it better to avoid mindfulness or mindlessness activities at these times because they're not distracting enough to stop my ruminating thoughts. You could also attach one of the to-do list tasks to your resting, for example by promising, "I will only do the washing up once I have spent ten minutes resting." This helps me feel confident that the task will get done and stops me from spending my rest time thinking about which of the many tasks I should do next.

Sometimes, resting feels frustrating because we believe we are the only ones who have to do it. Our social media feeds are full of work achievements, life events, holidays, and side hustles (another reason not to use social media as a rest activity). I promise you: Everyone needs rest. Those who avoid it are only going to burn themselves out in the long run.

Make sure there are activities in your Rest Bank that are fun and enjoyable, but don't avoid a particular type of rest just because it isn't exciting. It can be good to build a tolerance for things that are calm rather than exhilarating, to learn how to be still instead of always chasing a thrill.

How Do I Set Boundaries around My Energy Use?

Setting—and enforcing—boundaries isn't easy, especially if you've spent a long time saying "yes" to everything and letting everyone except yourself get a say in how your energy is used.

Hopefully, *Pace Yourself* has given you some ideas for the kinds of boundaries you might put in place. If your pacing diary revealed that most of your feelings of fatigue directly follow the times when you spend a lot of emotional energy solving others' problems, it indicates that you probably need to restrict how this energy is used. Or you might have noticed that you tend to overcommit to new fitness programs, pushing your body to physical exhaustion instead of gradually doing more exercise—in this case, you need to set *yourself* a boundary.

When you've identified some boundaries, it's important that you communicate them clearly to the people around you. You may think that they're obvious, that they don't need stating, but people aren't always very attuned to what matters to others. If it's taken us a lot of effort to realize what our boundaries are, how can we expect anyone else to know them without our input?

Despite all best efforts, however, sometimes boundaries have to be crossed. Compromises will need to be made. If you've had to be flexible on one occasion, don't consider this a failure on your part or a lack of self-respect. Instead, reflect on what you've learned about the boundary itself. Does it need adjusting? Were you surprised by the way you felt after the compromise? Do you need to better explain your boundary so that it isn't ignored in future?

How Do I Know If I'm Doing Too Much, Too Soon?

It's perfectly normal to feel tired after a busy day, or to want to rest more some days than others—I love a weekend spent at home, doing very little, reading a good book, and binge-watching *Gilmore Girls*. Ideally, you want to have a good balance of activity and rest across each day, but that doesn't mean every day has to be the same.

However, if your day-to-day activities are unsustainable and you find yourself back in a boom-and-bust pattern, needing to cancel plans and spend a lot more time resting to make up for overexertion the previous day, then you're probably doing more than you should be. Remember the quote about pacing from chapter 8: "I used to take two steps forward and three steps back, and now I take one step at a time."

Help! I've Had a Relapse / My Symptoms Are Worse—What Do I Do?

Relapsing is a scary, difficult thing to deal with. Sometimes there is a clear cause—I think my worst relapse was a result of very low levels of vitamin D, though I'll never know for certain—but there isn't always an explanation.

When any of my symptoms get suddenly worse, or new symptoms appear, I always see my doctor just to check that there isn't anything else going on.

Then, I go back to my vital pace. The amount of activity I include depends on the severity of my relapse, but I try to remind myself that this pace is temporary. I know I can pace up in the future, when I am ready.

Still, after my relapse it took some time for me to come to terms with the change in my energy levels and to accept that, for now, I'd have to reduce my hours at work and the time I spent with friends. I felt real grief at the unwanted change to my pace of life.

I think the thing that helped me most was the support of my family and of the ME/CFS community I found online. Whatever your illness, I'm sure there are charities or Facebook groups designed to help people like you. Sharing problems with strangers felt a little awkward at first, but I'm extremely grateful to have had a safe, supportive place to turn to.

Is It Possible to Pace during Big Life Events?

I've had ME/CFS for more than a decade. In that time I've graduated from university, moved homes, lived through a pandemic, and got married. I really believe none of those things would have happened if I hadn't learned to pace myself, and how to adapt that pace when needed.

Predictable life events are easier to pace. In the run-up to my wedding, I was very careful not to overexert myself, but I also made sure that I was gradually using more physical energy, pacing up and toward the activity I was most looking forward to: dancing with my husband and our friends to our favorite music. I spent so much time on the dance floor that night, I missed the arrival of a lot of evening guests! Sure, my legs hurt the next morning and I only just made it in time for the serving of breakfast, but I had avoided the dreaded post-exertional malaise.

When big events suddenly arise, it can be much harder to control your activity and thus your energy levels. Sometimes, you'll find yourself moving at a boom-and-bust pace just to keep up with the changes in your situation. In these cases, noticing your feelings of energy is key to avoiding burnout and overwhelming exhaustion. Take rest wherever you can and try to reduce the energy demands of your activity as much as possible. If you have to lower your standards during this time to stop yourself from burning out, do so.

What Tools or Equipment Will Help Me Pace Myself?

Some people like to use technology to help them pace, while others prefer nothing more than a pen and paper. It's worth experimenting with different options to figure out what works best for you.

When keeping a pacing diary, you could try using a calendar app to log every activity, along with notes about its impact on your energy levels. I like to use a timer app called Toggl to track how long I spend doing one activity, then I write this down in a physical diary with some information about my feelings of energy. I choose to create my own diary in a dotted notebook, a bit like a bullet journal (if you haven't heard of bullet journaling, search the term on Google or social media, but be warned: You may end up spending a lot of money on highlighters and brush pens!).

I have started experimenting with keeping a verbal diary, recording my thoughts for the day on my phone's voice note app. It isn't a particularly useful way to see trends in my energy use, mainly because I really don't like listening to the sound of my own voice, but I've found it a good way to explore ideas and talk through feelings before I make a note of them elsewhere.

I use the same physical notebook when designing my pace of life and to keep track of my goals and milestones (chapter 10).

You don't have to keep an ongoing diary in order to pace. If you find it easier to go about your life without planning each activity or writing down every time you feel fatigued, that's fine, too. Pacing is just about having a healthy balance between your energy and your activity—how you achieve that is really up to you.

I Know I'm in a Boom-and-Bust Lifestyle, but Isn't the "Boom" Worth the "Bust"?

In the beginning, maybe. The first few times you go on the boom-and-bust roller coaster, the bust is generally minimal. You might not even notice it, because you're still feeling the excitement and thrill of the boom.

But you've picked up this book for a reason. You know your current pace of life is unsustainable.

The thing is, when we're climbing the boom, we're only looking up. We don't see what's being left behind—the weeknights and weekends that suffer, the time with your family and friends, your own health and well-being—nor do we see the inevitable drop that awaits. We're too busy looking at the bright blue sky above us.

When you spend so long staring at the summit, you can't help imagining how you'll feel when you reach it. It will all be worth it when you get to the top, you think. All that matters is being there, looking out, knowing you achieved what you set out to do.

If, for a brief moment, we do consider what happens after, we tell ourselves that this time there will be no bust. This time, the high will remain. This goal, we tell ourselves, is the one that will change the pace of our lives. This achievement will flatten the track and we'll stay at this level of happiness, of success, from now on.

It won't. The only way to prevent the roller coaster from descending is to step off the ride.

The Real-Time Pacing Diary

When first considering pacing, it's important to understand your current activity and energy levels. You might choose to monitor these using a real-time pacing diary [chapter 4]. An example of this diary can be found below. Don't feel like you have to follow this to the letter: If it's more natural for you to write less or more, do so. The important thing is that you begin noticing your energy levels and write down any key activities that affect them.

On Waking

- How do you feel about your levels of emotional, mental, and physical energy for the day ahead?
- Do you feel emotionally rested?
- Do you feel mentally rested?
- Do you feel physically rested?

Activity	Feelings of energy		
	Emotional	Mental	Physical
8:00 a.m.–2:00 p.m Breakfast: coffee with toast and jam	Dreading big meeting later.	A little sluggish.	Well-rested.
8:00 a.m.–8:20 a.m. Shower	—	Couldn't remember if I'd shampooed once or twice = brain fog!	—
9:00 a.m.–9:30 a.m. Started work, mostly emails	Getting anxious about my bit in morning meeting.	Taking me longer than normal to reply to emails.	—
9:30 a.m.–10:00 a.m. Call with colleague	Helped calm nerves a little.	—	Did my call while walking around the house.
10:00 a.m.–12:00 p.m. Meeting	Draining until my part, then after I'd finished I felt quite calm.	I had saved myself a lot of mental energy by preparing note cards in advance.	—

Activity	Feelings of energy		
	Emotional	Mental	Physical
12:00 p.m.– 1:00 p.m. Lunch: sandwich, crisps, chocolate bar. Fruit juice and another cup of coffee	Feeling too tired to chat with housemates during my lunch break so took myself outside for a quiet meal on a park bench	–	Walking to and from the park feels like it actually gave me more energy!
1:00 p.m.– 3:15 p.m. Working on design brief (solo work, headphones on)	–	I find this sort of work much less mentally taxing than answering emails	Took a few breaks to stretch my legs
15:30 p.m.– 5:00 p.m. Answering more emails and calling clients who hadn't responded to my questions in over a week	–	Boring and mentally unstimulating, which was more tiring than work that requires more effort but is at least interesting!	–
5:30 p.m.– 6:30 p.m. Weekly supermarket shop	·Forgot my shopping list so irritable and frustrated (at myself, but also at annoying slow drivers en route)	Clearly tired— bought the wrong milk and forgot to get bread	Driving and walking around the shop tired me out—don't want to have to stand for ages cooking tea tonight
7:00 p.m.– 7:30 p.m. Evening meal: frozen pizza	Feeling a little guilty about not eating something healthier	–	–
7:30 p.m.– 8:45 p.m. Scrolled on TikTok for way too long	Still frustrated with myself for forgetting my list and probably overspending at the supermarket. On reflection, I also feel like I did badly in the meeting	Got a bit carried away thinking about potential side hustles and used a lot of energy coming up with new business ventures I'll never actually implement	Should probably have done some exercise or yoga but am way too tired

Activity	Feelings of energy		
	Emotional	Mental	Physical
9:00 p.m.–11:30 p.m. Watched five episodes of *Friends* back-to-back even though I should have gone to bed earlier	More guilt, but can't ever feel too bad while watching this show	—	—

Before Bed

- How do you feel about where you spent your emotional, mental, and physical energy today?
- Do you feel like you exhausted your emotional energy today?
- Do you feel like you exhausted your mental energy today?
- Do you feel like you exhausted your physical energy today?

The Reconstructive Pacing Diary

If a real-time diary isn't feasible, you might try completing a reconstructive diary for the first two weeks of pacing. This involves sitting down at the same time every day to reflect on your activity and feelings of energy.

This diary is loosely based on the one developed by Daniel Kahneman and colleagues in 2004. You may choose to complete it at any time of day, but I'd suggest either early in the morning or in the evening. If you decide to write your diary in the morning, fill out the questions in line with the previous day's activities.

Morning (From Waking until Noon)

- Roughly what time did you wake up?
- What did you eat for breakfast?
- What activities did you do?

Activity	Impact on your feelings of energy		
	Emotional	Mental	Physical

Afternoon (From Noon until 6:00 p.m.)

- What did you eat for lunch?
- What activities did you do?

Activity	Impact on your feelings of energy		
	Emotional	Mental	Physical

Evening (From 6:00 p.m. until You Go to Bed)

- What did you eat for your evening meal?
- What activities did you do?
- What time did you go to sleep?

Activity	Impact on your feelings of energy		
	Emotional	Mental	Physical

Sleep Diary

If you're concerned about your sleep, it's recommended that you speak to a doctor. If you can, monitor your sleep in the week or so leading up to your appointment. This way you'll be able to provide your doctor with specific details about your situation.

Alongside your pacing diary, you may want to answer the following questions each day:

1. What time did you go to bed?
2. What time did you get out of bed?
3. Did you wake up in the middle of the night? How often, and how long were you awake?
4. Did you have a nap during the day? How many, and how long did you sleep?
5. How do you feel the quality of your sleep was?
6. Did you drink anything caffeinated or alcoholic or smoke tobacco? How much and at what time of day?
7. Did you do any exercise?
8. Did you take any medication?

Chronotype Questionnaire

The below morningness/eveningness questionnaire was designed to determine whether you have a morning, evening, or intermediate chronotype [chapter six]. It is based on the questionnaire developed by J. A. Horne and O. Ostberg for their 1976 paper "A Self-Assessment Questionnaire to Determine Morningness-Eveningness in Human Circadian Rhythms." It's worth pointing out that this was not designed with ME/CFS or long COVID in mind, so some of the questions may not suit people with these conditions.

Answer each question as honestly as you can, circling the number to the right of your answer. At the end of the questionnaire, you'll need to add up these numbers to reveal a score that indicates your chronotype.

Roughly what time would you get up if you were entirely free to plan your day?

5:00–6:30 a.m.	5
6:30–7:45 a.m.	4
7:45–9:45 a.m.	3
9:45–11:00 a.m.	2
11:00 a.m.–12 noon	1

Roughly what time would you go to bed if you were entirely free to plan your evening?

8:00–9:00 p.m.	5
9:00–10:15 p.m.	4
10:15 p.m.–12:30 a.m.	3
12:30–1:45 a.m.	2
1:45–3:00 a.m.	1

If you normally have to get up at a specific time each morning, how much do you depend on an alarm clock to wake you?

Not at all	4
Slightly	3
Somewhat	2
Very much	1

How easy do you normally find it to get up in the morning?

Not at all easy   1

Not very easy   2

Fairly easy   3

Very easy   4

How alert do you feel during the first half hour after waking up in the morning?

Not at all alert   1

Slightly alert   2

Fairly alert   3

Very alert   4

How hungry do you feel during the first half hour after waking up in the morning?

Not at all hungry   1

Slightly hungry   2

Fairly hungry   3

Very hungry   4

How tired do you feel during the first half hour after waking up?

Very tired   1

Fairly tired   2

Fairly refreshed   3

Very refreshed   4

What time would you go to bed, compared to your usual bedtime, if you have no plans or commitments the following day?

Slightly or no later than normal   4

Less than one hour later   3

One to two hours later   2

More than two hours later   1

Imagine you've told a friend that you want to do some physical
exercise. They suggest you plan to exercise for one hour, twice
a week, and that the best time for them is between 7:00 and
8:00 a.m. Thinking about nothing other than your own sleep-wake
rhythm (so ignoring your actual ability to exercise), how do you
think you would perform at that hour?

I would be in good form 4

I would be in reasonable form 3

I would find it difficult 2

I would find it very difficult 1

Roughly what time in the evening do you start to feel tired and
need to go to bed?

8:00–9:00 p.m. 5

9:00–10:15 p.m. 4

10:15 p.m.–12:45 a.m. 3

12:45–2:00 a.m. 2

2:00–3:00 a.m. 1

Imagine you have to take a two-hour test that you know is going to
be mentally exhausting. You want to be at your peak performance.
Thinking about nothing other than your own sleep-wake rhythm
and alertness (so ignoring your actual cognitive ability), which one
of these four testing times would you choose?

8:00–10:00 a.m. 6

11:00 a.m.–1:00 p.m. 4

3:00–5:00 p.m. 2

7:00–9:00 p.m. 0

If you got into bed at 11:00 p.m., how tired would you be?

Not at all tired 0

A little tired 2

Fairly tired 3

Very tired 5

Imagine you have gone to bed several hours later than usual, but you know you have no commitments the next day nor any reason to get up at any particular time in the morning. Your usual alarm, if you have one, is switched off. Which one of the following are you most likely to do?

I would wake up at my usual time, but will not fall back to sleep   4

I would wake up at my usual time and would doze thereafter   3

I would wake up at my usual time, but would fall back to sleep again . . .   2

I would not wake up until later than usual   1

For some reason, you have to carry out a night watch between 4:00 and 6:00 a.m. You have to remain awake during this time, but you have no other commitments the next day. Which option out of the following would suit you best?

I would not go to bed until the watch is over   1

I would take a nap before the watch, then sleep after   2

I would have a good sleep before the watch, then nap after   3

I would sleep only before the watch   4

You have to do two hours of hard physical work, but you are entirely free to plan your day around this commitment. Thinking about nothing other than your own sleep-wake rhythm (so ignoring your actual ability to complete physical tasks), which one of the following times would you choose?

8:00–10:00 a.m.   4

11:00 a.m.–1:00 p.m.   3

3:00–5:00 p.m.   2

7:00–9:00 p.m.   1

Imagine you've told a different friend that you want to do some physical exercise. They suggest you plan to exercise for one hour, twice a week, and that the best time for them is between 10:00 and 11:00 p.m. Thinking about nothing other than your own sleep-wake rhythm (so ignoring your actual ability to exercise), how do you think you would perform at that hour?

I would be in good form   1

I would be in reasonable form   2

I would find it difficult   3

I would find it very difficult   4

If you could choose your own work hours, what start time would be preferable? Assume that your job is a five-hour day, including breaks, and is interesting and well paid.

Starting your work day between 4:00 and 8:00 a.m. 5

Starting your work day between 8:00 and 9:00 a.m. 4

Starting your work day between 9:00 a.m. and 2:00 p.m. 3

Starting your work day between 2:00 and 5:00 p.m. 2

Starting your work day between 5:00 p.m. and 4:00 a.m. 1

Roughly, during what time of the day do you usually feel your best?

5:00–8:00 a.m. 5

8:00–10:00 a.m. 4

10:00am–5:00 p.m. 3

5:00–10:00 p.m. 2

10:00pm–5:00 a.m. 1

In your opinion, which of the two chronotypes—"morning type" and "evening type"—do you consider yourself to be?

Definitely a morning type 6

More a morning type than an evening type 4

More an evening type than a morning type 2

Definitely an evening type 1

Total points: _____

Interpreting Your Result

The potential score for this questionnaire ranges from 16 to 86. A score of 41 and below suggests you are an "evening type," while a score of 59 and above indicates a "morning type." Scoring between 42 and 58 indicates an "intermediate type."

Notes

~~~~~~~~~~

Introduction

1. World Health Organization (1998). WHOQOL User Manual. https://www.who.int/publications/i/item/WHO-HIS-HSI-Rev.2012-3.
2. Rauch, H. G., Schönbächler, G., & Noakes, T. D. (2013). "Neural Correlates of Motor Vigor and Motor Urgency During Exercise." *Sports Medicine* (Auckland, N.Z.) 43(4), 227–241. https://doi.org/10.1007/s40279-013-0025-1.
3. Hampson, D. B., St. Clair Gibson, A., Lambert, M. I., et al. (2001). "The Influence of Sensory Cues on the Perception of Exertion During Exercise and Central Regulation of Exercise Performance." *Sports Med* 31, 935–952. https://doi.org/10.2165/00007256-200131130-00004.
4. Dolan, P. (2015). *Happiness by Design*. Penguin.
5. Koepp, M. J., Gunn, R. N., Lawrence, A. D., Cunningham, V. J., Dagher, A., Jones, T., Brooks, D. J., Bench, C. J. & Grasby, P. M. (1998). "Evidence for Striatal Dopamine Release During a Video Game." *Nature* 393(6682), 266–268. https://doi.org/10.1038/30498.
6. Lomas, T. (2021). "Life Balance and Harmony: Wellbeing's Golden Thread." *International Journal of Wellbeing* 11(1), 50–68. https://doi.org/10.5502/ijw.v11i1.1477.

Chapter One—
Highs and Lows: Emotional Energy

1. Ekman, P. (1992). "An Argument for Basic Emotions." *Cognition and Emotion* 6(3/4), 169–200. https://doi.org/10.1080/02699939208411068.
2. Burnet, D. (2023). *Emotional Ignorance: Lost and Found in the Science of Emotion*. Guardian Faber Publishing.
3. Russell J. A. (2003). "Core Affect and the Psychological Construction of Emotion." *Psychological Review* 110(1), 145–172. https://doi.org/10.1037/0033-295x.110.1.145.

4. Lim, N. (2016). "Cultural Differences in Emotion: Differences in Emotional Arousal Level Between the East and the West." *Integrative Medicine Research* 5(2), 105–109. https://doi.org/10.1016/j.imr.2016 .03.004.

5. Lu, L., Gilmour, R. (2004). "Culture and Conceptions of Happiness: Individual Oriented and Social Oriented Swb." *Journal of Happiness Studies* 5, 269–291. https://doi.org/10.1007/s10902-004-8789-5.

6. Price, C. J. & Hooven, C. (2018). "Interoceptive Awareness Skills for Emotion Regulation: Theory and Approach of Mindful Awareness in Body-Oriented Therapy (MABT)." *Front. Psychol.* 9:798. https://doi .org/10.3389/fpsyg.2018.00798.

7. Mort, S. (2022). *A Manual for Being Human.* Simon & Schuster UK.

8. Dumas, G., Nadel, J., Soussignan, R., Martinerie, J., Garnero, L. (2010). "Inter-Brain Synchronization during Social Interaction." *PLOS ONE* 5(8): e12166. https://doi.org/10.1371/journal.pone.0012166.

9. De Hert, S. (2020). "Burnout in Healthcare Workers: Prevalence, Impact and Preventative Strategies." *Local and Regional Anesthesia* 13, 171–183. https://doi.org/10.2147/LRA.S240564.

10. Grandey, A. A., Fisk, G. M. & Steiner, D. D. (2005). "Must 'Service with a Smile' Be Stressful? The Moderating Role of Personal Control for American and French Employees." *Journal of Applied Psychology* 90(5), 893–904. https://doi.org/10.1037/0021-9010.90.5.893.

11. Ekemezie, C. (2021). "Why It's Hard for People of Colour to be Themselves at Work." BBC. https://www.bbc.com/worklife/article /20210119-why-its-hard-for-people-of-colour-to-be-themselves-at-work.

12. Deligkaris, P., Panagopoulou, E., Montgomery, A. J. & Masoura, E. (2014). "Job Burnout and Cognitive Functioning: A Systematic Review." *Work & Stress* 28:2, 107–123. https://researchportal.northumbria.ac.uk/en /publications/job-burnout-and-cognitive-functioning-a-systematic-review.

13. Ibid.

14. Ibid.

15. *Medical News Today* (2020). "Why Might a Person Cry for No Reason?" medicalnewstoday.com/articles/crying-for-no-reason.

16. Greenberg D. B. (2002). "Clinical Dimensions of Fatigue." Primary care companion to the *Journal of Clinical Psychiatry* 4(3), 90–93. https:// doi.org/10.4088/pcc.v04n0301.

17. Campaign to End Loneliness N.D.. "Facts and Statistics About Loneliness." https://www.campaigntoendloneliness.org/facts-and -statistics/ (Accessed July 2023).

18. Ibid.

19. National Institute for Health and Care Excellence (2021). "Myalgic Encephalomyelitis (or Encephalopathy)/Chronic Fatigue Syndrome: Diagnosis and Management." nice.org.uk/guidance/ng206.

20. Vernon, S. D., Hartle, M., Sullivan, K., Bell, J., Abbaszadeh, S., Unutmaz, D. & Bateman, L. (2023). "Post-Exertional Malaise Among People with Long COVID Compared to Myalgic Encephalomyelitis/ Chronic Fatigue Syndrome (ME/CFS)." *Work* 74(4), 1179–1186. https:// doi.org/10.3233/WOR-220581.

21. Parkinson, B. & Simons, G. (2009). "Affecting Others: Social Appraisal and Emotion Contagion in Everyday Decision Making." *Personality & Social Psychology Bulletin* 35(8), 1071–1084. https://doi.org/10.1177 /0146167209336611.

22. Reed, J., Ones, D. S. (2006). "The Effect of Acute Aerobic Exercise on Positive Activated Affect: A Meta-Analysis." *Psychology of Sport and Exercise* 7:5, 477–514, ISSN 1469–0292, https://doi.org/10.1016/j .psychsport.2005.11.003.

23. Magnuson, C. D. & Barnett, L. A. (2013). "The Playful Advantage: How Playfulness Enhances Coping with Stress." *Leisure Sciences* 35:2, 129–144, https://doi.org/10.1080/01490400.2013.761905.

24. Brown, B. (2010). *The Gifts of Imperfection*. Hazelden.

25. Bandura, A. (2010). "Self-Efficacy." In: Weiner, I. B., Craighead, W. E. (eds). *The Corsini Encyclopedia of Psychology*. https://doi .org/10.1002/9780470479216.corpsy0836.

Chapter Two—
Mind Over Matter: Mental Energy

1. Tseng, J. & Poppenk, J. (2020). "Brain Meta-State Transitions Demarcate Thoughts Across Task Contexts Exposing the Mental Noise of Trait Neuroticism." *Nat Commun* 11, 3480. https://doi.org /10.1038/s41467-020-17255-9.

2. Killingsworth, M. A., Gilbert, D. T. (2010). "A Wandering Mind Is an Unhappy Mind." *Science* 330, 932. https://doi.org/10.1126/science.1192439.

3. Kahneman, D. (1973). *Attention and Effort*. Prentice-Hall Inc.

4. Norton, M. I., Mochon, D. & Ariely, D. (July 2012). "The IKEA Effect: When Labor Leads to Love." *Journal of Consumer Psychology* 22/3, 453–460. https://doi.org/10.1016/j.jcps.2011.08.002.

5. Boksem, M. A. S., Tops, M. (2008). "Mental Fatigue: Costs and Benefits." *Brain Research Reviews* 59(1), 125–139. https://doi.org/10 .1016/j.brainresrev.2008.07.001.

6. Yeo, G. & Neal, A. (2008). "Subjective Cognitive Effort: A Model of States, Traits, and Time." *Journal of Applied Psychology* 93, 617–631. http://doi.org/10.1037/0021-9010.93.3.617.

7. Ramachandran, V. (2021). "Stanford Researchers Identify Four Causes for 'Zoom Fatigue' and Their Simple Fixes." news.stanford.edu/2021/02 /23/four-causes-zoom-fatigue-solutions.

8. Robinson, M. M. & Morsella, E. (2014). "The Subjective Effort of Everyday Mental Tasks: Attending, Assessing, and Choosing." *Motiv Emot* 38, 832–843. https://doi.org/10.1007/s11031-014-9441-2.

9. Csikszentmihalyi, M. (1990). *Flow: The Psychology of Optimal Experience.* Harper.

10. Molden, D. C., Hui, C. M., Scholer, A. A., Meier, B. P., Noreen, E. E., D'Agostino, P. R. & Martin, V. (2012). "Motivational versus Metabolic Effects of Carbohydrates on Self-Control." *Psychological Science* 23(10), 1137–1144. https://doi.org/10.1177/0956797612439069.

11. Kurzban, R., Duckworth, A., Kable, J. W. & Myers, J. (2013). "An Opportunity Cost Model of Subjective Effort and Task Performance." *Behavioral and Brain Sciences* 36(6), 661–679. https://doi.org/10.1017/S0140525X12003196.

12. Zhou, Y., Danbolt, N. C. (2014). "Glutamate as a Neurotransmitter in the Healthy Brain." *J Neural Transm* 121, 799–817. https://doi.org/10.1007/s00702-014-1180-8.

13. Wiehler, A., Branzoli, F., Adanyeguh, I., Mochel, F., & Pessiglione, M. (2022). "A Neuro-Metabolic Account of Why Daylong Cognitive Work Alters the Control of Economic Decisions." *Current Biology* 32(16), 3564–3575: e5, ISSN 0960-9822, https://doi.org/10.1016/j.cub.2022.07.010.

14. Blain, B., Hollard, G. & Pessiglione, M. (2016). "Neural Mechanisms Underlying the Impact of Daylong Cognitive Work on Economic Decisions." *PNAS* 113, 6967–6972. https://www.pnas.org/doi/pdf/10.1073/pnas.1520527113.

15. Faber, L. G., Maurits, N. M., & Lorist, M. M. (2012). "Mental Fatigue Affects Visual Selective Attention." *PLOS ONE* 7(10), e48073. https://doi.org/10.1371/journal.pone.0048073.

16. Chatterjee, R. (2018). *The Stress Solution.* Penguin Life.

17. International Labour Organization (2013). "Case Study: Karoshi: Death from Overwork." ilo.org/global/topics/safety-and-health-at-work/resources-library/publications/WCMS_211571/lang—en/index.htm.

18. Skarpsno, E. S., Nilsen, T. I. L., Sand, T., Hagen, K. & Mork, P. J. (2020). "Work-Related Mental Fatigue, Physical Activity and Risk of Insomnia Symptoms: Longitudinal Data from the Norwegian HUNT Study." *Behavioral Sleep Medicine* 18(4), 488–499. https://doi.org/10.1080/15402002.2019.1614927.

19. Bang, H., & Reio, T. G. (2017). "Examining The Role of Cynicism in the Relationships Between Burnout and Employee Behavior." *Revista de Psicología del Trabajo y de las Organizaciones* 33(3), 217–227, ISSN 1576-5962, https://doi.org/10.1016/j.rpto.2017.07.002.

20. Chopra, D. (1994). *The Seven Spiritual Laws of Success.* New World Library.

21. Agrawal, M., Mattar, M. G., Cohen, J. D. & Daw, N. D. (2022). "The Temporal Dynamics of Opportunity Costs: A Normative Account of Cognitive Fatigue and Boredom." *Psychological Review* 129(3), 564–585. https://doi.org/10.1037/rev0000309.

22. Raichle, M. E. (2015). "The Brain's Default Mode Network." *Annual Review of Neuroscience* 38(1), 433–447. https://doi.org/10.1146/annurev-neuro-071013-014030.

23. Tang, Y., Bruya, B. (2017). "Mechanisms of Mind-Body Interaction and Optimal Performance." *Frontiers in Psychology* 8. https://doi.org/10.3389/fpsyg.2017.00647.

24. O'Mara, S. (2023). "In Praise of 'Mindlessness'—Escaping Self." brainpizza.substack.com/p/in-praise-of-mindlessness-escaping.

25. Bar, M. (2022). *Mindwandering*. Bloomsbury Publishing PLC.

26. Murakami, H. (2009). *What I Talk About When I Talk About Running*. Vintage.

27. Farrimond, S. (2020). *The Science of Living*. DK.

28. Hilditch, C. J., Dorrian, J. & Banks, S. (2016). "Time to Wake Up: Reactive Countermeasures to Sleep Inertia." *Industrial health* 54(6), 528–541. https://doi.org/10.2486/indhealth.2015-0236.

Chapter Three—In Motion: Physical Energy

1. Caspersen, C. J., Powell, K. E. & Christenson, G. M. (1985). "Physical Activity, Exercise, and Physical Fitness: Definitions and Distinctions for Health-Related Research." *Public Health Reports* (Washington, DC: 1974) 100(2), 126–131. https://www.ncbi.nlm.nih.gov/pmc/articles/PMC1424733/.

2. Ibid.

3. von Loeffelholz, C., Birkenfeld, A. L. (2000; updated November 25, 2022). "Non-Exercise Activity Thermogenesis in Human Energy Homeostasis." In: Feingold, K. R., Anawalt, B., Blackman, M. R., et al. (eds). *Endotext* [Internet]. South Dartmouth (MA): MDText.com, Inc. https://www.ncbi.nlm.nih.gov/books/NBK279077/.

4. Compendium of Physical Activities (2011). "11—Occupation." sites.google.com/site/compendiumofphysicalactivities/Activity-Categories/occupation.

5. Zitting, K. M., Vujovic, N., Yuan, R. K., Isherwood, C. M., Medina, J. E., Wang, W., Buxton, O. M., Williams, J. S., Czeisler, C. A. & Duffy, J. F. (2018). "Human Resting Energy Expenditure Varies with Circadian Phase." *Current Biology* 28(22), 3685–3690.e3. https://doi.org/10.1016/j.cub.2018.10.005.

6. Marcora, S. M. & Staiano, W. (2010). "The Limit to Exercise Tolerance in Humans: Mind Over Muscle?" *European Journal of Applied*

Physiology 109(4), 763–770. https://doi.org/10.1007s00421-010 -1418-6.

7. Martin, K., Staiano, W., Menaspà, P., Hennessey, T., Marcora, S., Keegan, R., Thompson, K. G., Martin, D., Halson, S. & Rattray, B. (2016). "Superior Inhibitory Control and Resistance to Mental Fatigue in Professional Road Cyclists." *PLOS ONE* 11(7), e0159907. https://doi.org /10.1371/journal.pone.0159907.

8. Blanchfield, A., Hardy, J. & Marcora, S. (2014). "Non-Conscious Visual Cues Related to Affect and Action Alter Perception of Effort and Endurance Performance." *Frontiers in Human Neuroscience* 8, 967. https://doi.org/10.3389/fnhum.2014.00967.

9. Stoate, I., Wulf, G. & Lewthwaite, R. (2012). "Enhanced Expectancies Improve Movement Efficiency in Runners." *Journal of Sports Sciences* 30(8), 815–823. https://doi.org/10.1080/02640414.2012.671533.

10. Mak, K. K., Ho, S. Y., Lo, W. S., et al. (2011). "Prevalence of Exercise and Non-Exercise Physical Activity in Chinese Adolescents." *Int J Behav Nutr Phys Act* 8, 3. https://doi.org/10.1186/1479-5868-8-3.

11. Healy, G. N., Dunstan, D. W., Salmon, J., Cerin, E., Shaw, J. E., Zimmet, P. Z., Owen, N. (2007). "Objectively Measured Light-Intensity Physical Activity Is Independently Associated with 2-h Plasma Glucose." *Diabetes Care* 30(6): 1384–1389. https://doi.org/10.2337/dc07-0114.

12. Sothern, M.S., Loftin, M., Suskind, R.M. et al. (1999). "The Health Benefits of Physical Activity in Children and Adolescents: Implications for Chronic Disease Prevention." *Eur J Pediatr* 158, 271–274. https:// doi.org/10.1007/s004310051070.

13. Owen, N, Healy, G. N., Matthews, C. E., Dunstan, D. W. (July 2010) "Too Much Sitting: The Population Health Science of Sedentary Behavior." *Exercise and Sport Sciences Reviews* 38(3), 105–113. https:// doi.org/10.1097%2FJES.0b013e3181e373a2.

14. Cheval, B., Maltagliati, S., Sieber, S., Cullati, S., Zou, L., Ihle, A., Kramer, A. F., Yu, Q., Sander, D., Boisgontier, M. P. (2022). "Better Subjective Sleep Quality Partly Explains the Association between Self-Reported Physical Activity and Better Cognitive Function." *Journal of Alzheimer's Disease,* 919–931. https://doi.org/10.3233/jad-215484.

15. Herring, M. P., Monroe, D. C., Kline, C. E., O'Connor, P. J. & MacDonncha, C. (2018). "Sleep Quality Moderates the Association Between Physical Activity Frequency and Feelings of Energy and Fatigue in Adolescents." *European Child & Adolescent Psychiatry* 27(11), 1425–1432. https://doi.org/10.1007/s00787-018-1134-z.

16. Lastella, M., Vincent, G. E., Duffield, R., Roach, G. D., Halson, S. L., Heales, L. J. & Sargent, C. (2018). "Can Sleep Be Used as an Indicator of Overreaching and Overtraining in Athletes?" *Frontiers in Physiology* 9, 436. https://doi.org/10.3389/fphys.2018.00436.

17. Mayo Clinic N.D. "Chronic Stress Puts Your Health at Risk." mayoclinic.org/healthy-lifestyle/stress-management/in-depth/stress/art-20046037 (Accessed July 2023).

18. Nieman, D. C. & Wentz, L. M. (2019). "The Compelling Link between Physical Activity and the Body's Defense System." *Journal of Sport and Health Science* 8(3), 201–217, ISSN 2095-2546. https://doi.org/10.1016/j.jshs.2018.09.009.

19. Nieman, D. C., Johanssen, L. M., Lee, J. W. & Arabatzis, K. (1990). "Infectious Episodes in Runners Before and After the Los Angeles Marathon." *Journal of Sports Medicine and Physical Fitness* 30(3), 316–328. https://pubmed.ncbi.nlm.nih.gov/2266764/.

20. Proschinger, S. & Freese, J. (2019). "Neuroimmunological and Neuroenergetic Aspects in Exercise-Induced Fatigue." *Exercise Immunology Review* 25, 8–19. http://doi.org/10.13140/RG.2.2.31212.62081.

21. NHS North Bristol N.D.. "Post-Viral Fatigue: A Guide to Management." nbt.nhs.uk/our-services/a-z-services/bristol-me-service/post-viral-fatigue-a-guide-management (Accessed July 2023).

22. Robb-Nicholson, L. C., Daltroy, L., Eaton, H., Gall, V., Wright, E., Hartley, L. H., Schur, P. H. & Liang, M. H. (1989). "Effects of Aerobic Conditioning in Lupus Fatigue: A Pilot Study." *British Journal of Rheumatology* 28(6), 500–505. https://doi.org/10.1093/rheumatology/28.6.500.

23. Mustian, K. M., Sprod, L. K., Janelsins, M., Peppone, L. J. & Mohile, S. (2012). "Exercise Recommendations for Cancer-Related Fatigue, Cognitive Impairment, Sleep Problems, Depression, Pain, Anxiety, and Physical Dysfunction: A Review." *Oncology & Hematology Review* 8(2), 81–88. https://doi.org/10.17925/ohr.2012.08.2.81.

24. Mostert, S. & Kesselring, J. (2002). "Effects of a Short-Term Exercise Training Program on Aerobic Fitness, Fatigue, Health Perception and Activity Level of Subjects with Multiple Sclerosis." *Multiple Sclerosis Journal* 8(2), 161–168. https://doi.org/10.1191/1352458502ms7790a.

25. National Institute for Health and Care Excellence (2021). "Myalgic Encephalomyelitis (or Encephalopathy)/Chronic Fatigue Syndrome: Diagnosis and Management." nice.org.uk/guidance/ng206.

26. Action for M.E (2019). "Five Year Big Survey." actionforme.org.uk/research-and-campaigns/five-year-big-survey/.

27. Forward-ME (2019). "Evaluation of a Survey Exploring the Experiences of Adults and Children with ME/CFS Who have Participated in CBT and GET Interventional Programs." https://www.meresearch.org.uk/wp-content/uploads/2019/04/Amended-Final-Consolidated-Report.pdf.

28. Antonelli, M. & Donelli, D. (2018). "Effects of Balneotherapy and Spa Therapy on Levels of Cortisol as a Stress Biomarker: A Systematic

Review." *Int J Biometeorol* 62, 913–924. https://doi.org/10.1007
/s00484-018-1504-8.

29. Metin, Z. G. & Ozdemir, L. (2016). "The Effects of Aromatherapy
Massage and Reflexology on Pain and Fatigue in Patients with
Rheumatoid Arthritis: A Randomized Controlled Trial." *Pain
Management Nursing* 17(2), 140–149, ISSN 1524-9042. https://doi.org
/10.1016/j.pmn.2016.01.004.

30. Mori, H., Ohsawa, H., Tanaka, T. H., Taniwaki, E., Leisman, G. & Nishijo,
K. (2004). "Effect of Massage on Blood Flow and Muscle Fatigue
Following Isometric Lumbar Exercise." *Medical Science Monitor:
International Medical Journal of Experimental and Clinical Research*
10(5), CR173–CR178. https://pubmed.ncbi.nlm.nih.gov/15114265/.

31. Massimini, F., Csikszentmihalyi, M. & Fave, A. D. (1988). "Flow and
Biocultural Evolution." In M. Csikszentmihalyi & I. S.
Csikszentmihalyi (eds.), *Optimal Experience: Psychological Studies of
Flow in Consciousness*, Cambridge University Press. 60–81.

32. Alexander, J. & Jarman, R. (2018). "The Pleasures of Reading
Non-Fiction." *Literacy* 52(2), 78–85. https://doi.org/10.1111/lit.12152.

33. Raymann, R. J., Swaab, D. F. & Van Someren, E. J. (2007). "Skin
Temperature and Sleep-Onset Latency: Changes with Age and
Insomnia." *Physiology & Behavior* 90(2-3), 257–266. https://doi.org
/10.1016/j.physbeh.2006.09.008.

34. Karadag, E., Baglama, S. S. (2019). "The Effect of Aromatherapy on
Fatigue and Anxiety in Patients Undergoing Hemodialysis Treatment:
A Randomized Controlled Study." *Holistic Nursing Practice* 33(4),
222–229. https://doi.org/10.1097/hnp.0000000000000334.

Chapter Four—
Define: Your Current Pace of Life

1. Gilbert, D. T. (2006). *Stumbling on Happiness*. Random House.
2. Grupe, D. W. & Nitschke, J. B. (2013). "Uncertainty and Anticipation in
Anxiety: An Integrated Neurobiological and Psychological
Perspective." *Nature Reviews. Neuroscience* 14(7), 488–501. https://doi
.org/10.1038/nrn3524.
3. Ravey, J. (2023). *Braintenance*. Macmillan.
4. Kahneman, D., Krueger, A. B., Schkade, D. A., Schwarz, N. & Stone, A.
A. (2004). "A Survey Method for Characterizing Daily Life Experience:
the Day Reconstruction Method." *Science* 306(5702), 1776–1780.
https://doi.org/10.1126/science.1103572.
5. Dolan, P. (2015). *Happiness by Design*. Penguin.

Chapter Five—Eating For Energy

1. Harrell, E. (2015). 'How 1% Performance Improvements Led to Olympic Gold'. hbr.org/2015/10/how-1-performance-improvements-led-to -olympic-gold.
2. Zhou, Z., Sun, B., Huang, S., et al. (2020). "Glycemic Variability: Adverse Clinical Outcomes and How to Improve It?" *Cardiovasc Diabetol* 19, 102. https://doi.org/10.1186/s12933-020-01085-6.
3. Inchauspé, J. (2022). *Glucose Revolution*. Short Books Ltd.
4. Giacco, R., Costabile, G., Della Pepa, G., Anniballi, G., Griffo, E., Mangione, A., Cipriano, P., Viscovo, D., Clemente, G., Landberg, R., Pacini, G., Rivellese, A. A. & Riccardi, G. (2014). "A Whole-Grain Cereal-Based Diet Lowers Postprandial Plasma Insulin and Triglyceride Levels in Individuals with Metabolic Syndrome." *Nutrition, Metabolism, and Cardiovascular Diseases: NMCD* 24(8), 837–844. https://doi.org/10.1016/j.numecd.2014.01.007.
5. Sonia, S., Witjaksono, F. & Ridwan, R. (2015). "Effect of Cooling of Cooked White Rice on Resistant Starch Content and Glycemic Response." *Asia Pacific Journal of Clinical Nutrition* 24(4), 620–625. https://doi.org/10.6133/apjcn.2015.24.4.13.
6. Muir, J. G. & O'Dea, K. (1992). "Measurement of Resistant Starch: Factors Affecting the Amount of Starch Escaping Digestion in Vitro." *American Journal of Clinical Nutrition* 56(1), 123–127. https://doi .org/10.1093/ajcn/56.1.123.
7. Layman, D. K., Boileau, R. A., Erickson, D. J., Painter, J. E., Shiue, H., Sather, C. & Christou, D. D. (2003). "A Reduced Ratio of Dietary Carbohydrate to Protein Improves Body Composition and Blood Lipid Profiles During Weight Loss in Adult Women." *Journal of Nutrition* 133(2), 411–417. https://doi.org/10.1093/jn/133.2.411.
8. Chen, H, Tao, Y, Li, M-D, et al. (2022). "Temporal Patterns of Energy Intake and Cognitive Function and Its Decline: A Community-Based Cohort Study in China." *Life Metab.* 1, 94–97. https://doi.org/10.1093 /lifemeta/loac011.
9. Mekary, R. A., Giovannucci, E., Willett, W. C., van Dam, R. M. & Hu, F. B. (2012). "Eating Patterns and Type 2 Diabetes Risk in Men: Breakfast Omission, Eating Frequency, and Snacking." *American Journal of Clinical Nutrition* 95(5), 1182–1189. https://doi.org/10.3945/ajcn .111.028209.
10. Bo, S., Musso, G., Beccuti, G., Fadda, M., Fedele, D., Gambino, R., Gentile, L., Durazzo, M., Ghigo, E. & Cassader, M. (2014). "Consuming More of Daily Caloric Intake at Dinner Predisposes to Obesity. A 6-Year Population-Based Prospective Cohort Study." *PLOS ONE* 9(9), e0108467. https://doi.org/10.1371/journal .pone.0108467.

11. Chen, Tao, Li, et al. (2022). "Temporal Patterns of Energy Intake and
     Cognitive Function and Its Decline: A Community-Based Cohort
     Study in China." *Life Metab.* 1, 94–97. https://doi.org/10.1093/lifemeta
     /loac011.

12. Vellanki, P. (2020). "Eat Breakfast Like a King and Dinner Like a
     Pauper." *Sci. Transl. Med.* 12, eabb0796. https://doi.org/10.1126
     /scitranslmed.abb0796.

13. Wilson, K. (2020). *How to Build a Healthy Brain.* Hodder & Stoughton.

14. Nafea, H., Abdelmegid, O., Qaddourah, S., Abdulwahab, Z., Moawad, J.
     & Shi, Z. (2021). "Higher Habitual Nuts Consumption Is Associated
     with Better Cognitive Function among Qatari Adults." *Nutrients*
     13(10), 3580. https://doi.org/10.3390/nu13103580.

15. Debono, M., Ghobadi, C., Rostami-Hodjegan, A., Huatan, H., Campbell,
     M. J., Newell-Price, J., Darzy, K., Merke, D. P., Arlt, W. & Ross, R. J.
     (2009). "Modified-Release Hydrocortisone to Provide Circadian
     Cortisol Profiles." *Journal of Clinical Endocrinology and Metabolism*
     94(5), 1548–1554. https://doi.org/10.1210/jc.2008-2380.

16. Rogers, P.J., Heatherley, S.V., Mullings, E.L. et al. (2013). "Faster but
     Not Smarter: Effects of Caffeine and Caffeine Withdrawal on Alertness
     and Performance." *Psychopharmacology* 226, 229–240. https://doi.org
     /10.1007/s00213-012-2889-4.

17. Kenny, R. A. (2022). *Age Proof.* Bonnier Books.

18. Armstrong, L. E., Ganio, M. S., Casa, D. J., Lee, E. C., McDermott, B. P.,
     Klau, J. F., Jimenez, L., Le Bellego, L., Chevillotte, E. & Lieberman,
     H. R. (2012). "Mild Dehydration Affects Mood in Healthy Young
     Women." *Journal of Nutrition* 142(2), 382–388. https://doi.org/10.3945
     /jn.111.142000.

19. Binks, H., E Vincent, G., Gupta, C., Irwin, C. & Khalesi, S. (2020).
     "Effects of Diet on Sleep: A Narrative Review." *Nutrients* 12(4), 936.
     https://doi.org/10.3390/nu12040936.

20. Richard, D. M., Dawes, M. A., Mathias, C. W., Acheson, A.,
     Hill-Kapturczak, N. & Dougherty, D. M. (2009). "L-Tryptophan: Basic
     Metabolic Functions, Behavioral Research and Therapeutic
     Indications." *International Journal of Tryptophan Research* 2, 45–60.
     https://doi.org/10.4137/ijtr.s2129.

21. Meng, X., Li, Y., Li, S., Zhou, Y., Gan, R. Y., Xu, D. P. & Li, H. B. (2017).
     "Dietary Sources and Bioactivities of Melatonin." *Nutrients* 9(4), 367.
     https://doi.org/10.3390/nu9040367.

22. Azzolino, D., Arosio, B., Marzetti, E., Calvani, R. & Cesari, M. (2020).
     "Nutritional Status as a Mediator of Fatigue and Its Underlying
     Mechanisms in Older People." *Nutrients* 12(2), 444. https://doi.org
     /10.3390/nu12020444.

23. Westergren A. (2008). "Nutrition and Its Relation to Mealtime Preparation, Eating, Fatigue and Mood Among Stroke Survivors After Discharge From Hospital—A Pilot Study." *Open Nursing Journal* 2, 15–20. https://doi.org/10.2174/1874434600802010015.

Chapter Six—
Sleep in Focus

1. National Heart, Lung, and Blood Institute N.D. "Insomnia: Diagnosis." nhlbi.nih.gov/health/insomnia/diagnosis (Accessed July 2023).
2. Siegel, J. M. (2005). "Clues to the Functions of Mammalian Sleep." *Nature* 437(7063), 1264–1271. https://doi.org/10.1038/nature04285.
3. Kenny, R. A. (2022). *Age Proof.* Bonnier Books.
4. Petit, J. M., Burlet-Godinot, S., Magistretti, P. J. & Allaman, I. (2015). "Glycogen Metabolism and the Homeostatic Regulation of Sleep." *Metabolic Brain Disease* 30(1), 263–279. https://doi.org/10.1007/s11011-014-9629-x.
5. Harvard Health Publishing (2020). "How Sleep Boosts Your Energy." health.harvard.edu/healthbeat/how-sleep-boosts-your-energy.
6. Ben Simon, E., Rossi, A., Harvey, A.G. et al. (2020). "Overanxious and Underslept." *Nat Hum Behav* 4, 100–110. https://doi.org/10.1038/s41562-019-0754-8.
7. Diekelmann, S., Born, J. (2010). "The Memory Function of Sleep." *Nat Rev Neurosci* 11, 114–126. https://doi.org/10.1038/nrn2762.
8. Walker, M. (2017). *Why We Sleep.* Allen Lane.
9. Kuriyama, K., Stickgold, R. & Walker, M. P. (2004). "Sleep-Dependent Learning and Motor-Skill Complexity." *Learning & Memory* 11(6), 705–713. https://doi.org/10.1101/lm.76304.
10. Jankowski, K. S. & Ciarkowska, W. (2008). "Diurnal Variation in Energetic Arousal, Tense Arousal, and Hedonic Tone in Extreme Morning and Evening Types." *Chronobiology International* 25(4), 577–595. https://doi.org/10.1080/07420520802261770.
11. Farrimond, S. *The Science of Living.*
12. Walker, M. Why We Sleep.
13. National Institutes of Health State of the Science Conference Statement (2005): "Manifestations and Management of Chronic Insomnia in Adults." *Sleep* 28(9), 1049–1057. https://doi.org/10.1093/sleep/28.9.1049.
14. Action for M. E. N.D. "Sleep and Rest," actionforme.org.uk/get-information/managing-your-symptoms/sleep-and-rest/ (Accessed July 2023).
15. Qanash, S., Al-Husayni, F., Falata, H., Halawani, O., Jahra, E., Murshed, B., Alhejaili, F., Ghabashi, A. & Alhashmi, H. (2021).

"Effect of Electronic Device Addiction on Sleep Quality and Academic Performance among Health Care Students: Cross-sectional Study." *JMIR Medical Education* 7(4), e25662. https://doi.org/10.2196/25662.

16. Stone, J. D., Rentz, L. E., Forsey, J., Ramadan, J., Markwald, R. R., Finomore, V. S., Galster, S. M., Rezai, A. & Hagen, J. A. (2020). "Evaluations of Commercial Sleep Technologies for Objective Monitoring during Routine Sleeping Conditions." *Nature and Science of Sleep* 12, 821–842. https://doi.org/10.2147/NSS.S270705.

17. Pacheco, D., Singh, A. (2023). "Alcohol and Sleep." sleepfoundation.org/nutrition/alcohol-and-sleep.

18. Mayo Clinic N.D. "Napping: Do's and Don'ts for Healthy Adults." mayoclinic.org/healthy-lifestyle/adult-health/in-depth/napping/art-20048319 (Accessed July 2023).

19. Kitamura, S., Katayose, Y., Nakazaki, K., Motomura, Y., Oba, K., Katsunuma, R., Terasawa, Y., Enomoto, M., Moriguchi, Y., Hida, A. & Mishima, K. (2016). "Estimating Individual Optimal Sleep Duration and Potential Sleep Debt." *Scientific Reports* 6, 35812. https://doi.org/10.1038/srep35812.

20. Trotti L. M. (2017). "Waking Up is the Hardest Thing I Do all Day: Sleep Inertia and Sleep Drunkenness." *Sleep Medicine Reviews* 35, 76–84. https://doi.org/10.1016/j.smrv.2016.08.005.

21. Hilditch, C. J. & McHill, A. W. (2019). "Sleep Inertia: Current Insights." *Nature and Science of Sleep* 11, 155–165. https://doi.org/10.2147/NSS.S188911.

22. Farrimond, S. (2020). *The Science of Living.*

23. Wust, S., Wolf, J., Hellhammer, D. H., Federenko, I., Schommer, N., Kirschbaum, C. (2000). "The Cortisol Awakening Response—Normal Values and Confounds." *Noise Health* 2, 79–88. https://www.noiseandhealth.org/text.asp?2000/2/7/79/31739.

24. Skurvydas, A., Zlibinaite, L., Solianik, R., Brazaitis, M., Valanciene, D., Baranauskiene, N., Majauskiene, D., Mickeviciene, D., Venckunas, T. & Kamandulis, S. (2020). "One Night of Sleep Deprivation Impairs Executive Function but Does not Affect Psychomotor or Motor Performance." *Biology of Sport* 37(1), 7–14. https://doi.org/10.5114/biolsport.2020.89936.

25. van der Helm, E., Gujar, N. & Walker, M. P. (2010). "Sleep Deprivation Impairs the Accurate Recognition of Human Emotions." *Sleep* 33(3), 335–342. https://doi.org/10.1093/sleep/33.3.335.

26. Yoo, SS., Hu, P., Gujar, N. et al. (2007). "A Deficit in the Ability to Form New Human Memories Without Sleep." *Nat Neurosci.* 10, 385–392 (2007). https://doi.org/10.1038/nn1851.

Chapter Seven—
Rest to Recharge

1. Center for Near Earth Object Studies N.D. "NEO Basics: Life on Earth." cneos.jpl.nasa.gov/about/life_on_earth.html (Accessed July 2023).
2. Maslach, C. & Leiter, M.P. (2016). "Understanding the Burnout Experience: Recent Research and its Implications for Psychiatry." *World Psychiatry* 15, 103. https://doi.org/10.1002%2Fwps.20311.
3. Bellezza, S., Paharia, N. & Keinan, A. (2017). "Conspicuous Consumption of Time: When Busyness and Lack of Leisure Time Become a Status Symbol." *Journal of Consumer Research* 44(1): 118–138. https://doi.org/10.1093/jcr/ucw076.
4. Yang, A. X., Hsee, C. K. (2019). "Idleness Versus Busyness." *Current Opinion in Psychology* 26, 15–18, ISSN 2352-250X. https://doi.org/10.1016/j.copsyc.2018.04.015.
5. Shulevitz, J. (2003). "Bring Back the Sabbath." *New York Times*. nytimes.com/2003/03/02/magazine/bring-back-the-sabbath.html.
6. Hammond, C. & Lewis, G. (2016). "The Rest Test: Preliminary Findings from a Large-Scale International Survey on Rest." In: Callard, F., Staines, K., Wilkes, J. (eds). *The Restless Compendium: Interdisciplinary Investigations of Rest and Its Opposites*. Basingstoke, UK, Palgrave Macmillan. Chapter 8. https://doi.org/10.1007/978-3-319-45264-7_8.
7. Statista (2023). "Smartphone Ownership Penetration in the United Kingdom (UK) in 2012–2023, by Age." statista.com/statistics/271851/smartphone-owners-in-the-united-kingdom-uk-by-age/.
8. Hammond, C. (2019). *The Art of Rest*. Canongate.

Chapter Eight—
Assess: Finding Your Vital Pace

1. Cox, D. L. (1999) "Chronic Fatigue Syndrome—An Occupational Therapy Program." *Occupational Therapy International* 6(1), 52–64. https://doi.org/10.1002/oti.88.
2. Maslow, A. H. (1943). "A Theory of Human Motivation." *Psychological Review* 50(4), 370–396. https://doi.org/10.1037/h0054346.
3. Francesco Cirillo N.D. "The Pomodoro® Technique." cirillocompany.de/pages/pomodoro-technique/ (Accessed July 2023).
4. Gifford, J., (2020). "The Rule of 52 and 17: It's Random, but It Ups Your Productivity." themuse.com/advice/the-rule-of-52-and-17-its-random-but-it-ups-your-productivity.
5. Eisenberger, R. (1992). "Learned Industriousness." *Psychological Review* 99(2), 248–267. https://doi.org/10.1037/0033-295X.99.2.248.

Chapter Nine—
The Pacing Lifestyle

1.   Ryan, R. M. & Deci, E. L. (2000). "Self-Determination Theory and the Facilitation of Intrinsic Motivation, Social Development, and Well-Being." *American Psychologist* 55(1), 68–78. https://doi .org/10.1037/0003-066X.55.1.68.
2.   Bandura, A (1977). "Self-Efficacy: Toward a Unifying Theory of Behavioral Change." *Psychological Review* 84(2): 191–215. https://doi .org/10.1037/0033-295X.84.2.191.
3.   Bandura, A (1977). "Self-Efficacy." *Psychological Review* 84(2).
4.   Fogg, BJ. (2021). *Tiny Habits*. Harvest.
5.   ScienceDaily / Society for Personality and Social Psychology (2014). "How We form Habits, Change Existing Ones." sciencedaily.com /releases/2014/08/140808111931.htm.
6.   Kirgios, E. L., Mandel, G. H., Park, Y., Milkman, K. L., Gromet, D. M., Kay, J. S., Duckworth, A. L. (2020). "Teaching Temptation Bundling to Boost Exercise: A Field Experiment." *Organizational Behavior and Human Decision Processes* 161, Supplement, 20–35. ISSN 0749-5978. https://doi.org/10.1016/j.obhdp.2020.09.003.
7.   Müller, T., Klein-Flügge, M. C., Manohar, S. G. et al. (2021). "Neural and Computational Mechanisms of Momentary Fatigue and Persistence in Effort-Based Choice." *Nat Commun* 12, 4593. https://doi.org/10.1038 /s41467-021-24927-7.
8.   Ravey, J. (2023). *Braintenance*. Macmillan.
9.   Kahneman, D. (2012). *Thinking, Fast and Slow*. Penguin.
10.   Stawarz, K., Gardner, B., Cox, A. et al. (2020). "What Influences the Selection of Contextual Cues When Starting a New Routine Behavior? An Exploratory Study." *BMC Psychol* 8, 29. https://doi.org/10.1186 /s40359-020-0394-9.
11.   Ferrari, J. R., O'Callaghan, J. & Newbegin, I. (2005). "Prevalence of Procrastination in the United States, United Kingdom, and Australia: Arousal and Avoidance Delays among Adults." *North American Journal of Psychology* 7(1), 1–6.
12.   Sirois, F. & Pychyl, T. (2013). "Procrastination and the Priority of Short-Term Mood Regulation: Consequences for Future Self." *Social and Personality Psychology Compass* 7(2), 115127.
13.   Shatz, I. N.D. "Procrastination Theories: The Psychological Frameworks for Explaining Procrastination." solvingprocrastination .com/procrastination-theories (Accessed July 2023).
14.   Wohl, M. J. A., Pychyl, T. A., Bennett, S. H. (2010). "I Forgive Myself, Now I Can Study: How Self-Forgiveness for Procrastinating Can Reduce

Future Procrastination." *Personality and Individual Differences* 48 (7), 803–808. ISSN 0191-8869. https://doi.org/10.1016/j.paid.2010.01.029.

15. van der Weiden, A., Benjamins, J., Gillebaart, M., Ybema, J. F. & de Ridder, D. (2020). "How to Form Good Habits? A Longitudinal Field Study on the Role of Self-Control in Habit Formation." *Frontiers in Psychology* 11, 560. https://doi.org/10.3389/fpsyg.2020.00560.

16. Burnett, D. (2016). *The Idiot Brain.* Guardian Faber Publishing.

Chapter Ten—
Small Steps to Big Goals

1. Epton, T., Currie, S. & Armitage, C. J. (2017). "Unique Effects of Setting Goals on Behavior Change: Systematic Review and Meta-Analysis." *Journal of Consulting and Clinical Psychology* 85(12), 1182–1198. https://doi.org/10.1037/ccp0000260.

2. Ravey, J. (2023) *Braintenance.* Macmillan.

3. Ibid.

4. Dweck, C. (2006). *Mindset.* Random House.

5. Huang, S., Jin, L. & Zhang, Y. (2017). "Step by Step: Sub-Goals as a Source of Motivation." *Organizational Behavior and Human Decision Processes* 141, 1–15. ISSN 0749-5978. https://doi.org/10.1016/j.obhdp.2017.05.001.

6. Gilbert, P., McEwan, K., Matos, M. & Rivis, A. (2011). "Fears of Compassion: Development of Three Self-Report Measures." *Psychology and Psychotherapy* 84(3), 239–255. https://doi.org/10.1348/147608310X526511.

7. Coultas, J. & van Leeuwen, E. (2015). "Conformity: Definitions, Types, and Evolutionary Grounding." In: Zeigler-Hill, V., Welling, L., Shackelford, T. (eds). *Evolutionary Perspectives on Social Psychology.* Springer, Cham. https://doi.org/10.1007/978-3-319-12697-5_15.

Chapter Eleven—
The Happiness of Energy

1. Diener, E., Heintzelman, S. J., Kushlev, K., Tay, L., Wirtz, D., Lutes, L. D. & Oishi, S. (2017). "Findings all Psychologists Should Know From the New Science on Subjective Well-Being." *Canadian Psychology/ Psychologie Canadienne* 58(2), 87–104. https://doi.org/10.1037/cap0000063.

2. Lyubomirsky, S., King, L. & Diener, E. (2005). "The Benefits of Frequent Positive Affect: Does Happiness Lead to Success?" *Psychological Bulletin* 131(6), 803–855. https://doi.org/10.1037/0033-2909.131.6.803.

3. Rao, T. S., Asha, M. R., Ramesh, B. N. & Rao, K. S. (2008).
    "Understanding Nutrition, Depression and Mental Illnesses." *Indian
    Journal of Psychiatry* 50(2), 77–82. https://doi.org/10.4103
    /0019-5545.42391.

4. Nutt, D., Wilson, S. & Paterson, L. (2008). "Sleep Disorders as Core
    Symptoms of Depression." *Dialogues in Clinical Neuroscience* 10(3),
    329–336. https://doi.org/10.31887/DCNS.2008.10.3/dnutt.

5. Triantafillou, S., Saeb, S., Lattie, E. G., Mohr, D. C. & Kording, K. P.
    (2019). "Relationship Between Sleep Quality and Mood: Ecological
    Momentary Assessment Study." *JMIR Mental Health* 6(3), e12613.
    https://doi.org/10.2196/12613.

6. Bridges, F. (2019). "Healthy Food Makes You Happy: Research Shows
    a Healthy Diet Improves Your Mental Health." *Forbes*. forbes.com/sites
    /francesbridges/2019/01/26/food-makes-you-happy-a-healthy-diet
    -improves-mental-health/.

7. Carver, C. S., Scheier, M. F. & Segerstrom, S. C. (2010). "Optimism."
    Clinical Psychology Review 30(7), 879–889. https://doi.org/10.1016
    /j.cpr.2010.01.006.

8. Delle Fave, A. (2014). "Eudaimonic and Hedonic Happiness." In: Michalos,
    A.C. (eds). *Encyclopedia of Quality of Life and Well-Being Research.*
    Springer, Dordrecht. https://doi.org/10.1007/978-94-007-0753-5_3778.

9. Kahneman, D. & Riis, J. (2005). "Living, and Thinking about it: Two
    Perspectives on Life." In: Huppert, F. A., Baylis, N. & Keverne, B. (eds)
    (2012). *The Science of Well-Being.* Oxford; online edn, Oxford Academic.
    https://doi.org/10.1093/acprof:oso/9780198567523.003.0011.

10. Dolan, P. *Happiness by Design.*

11. Action for Happiness (2020). "Happiness Habits—with Sonja
    Lyubomirsky." youtube.com/watch?v=qYmLTG03ZDo.

12. Berger, M. W. (2023). "Does more money correlate with greater
    happiness?" penntoday.upenn.edu/news/does-more-money-correlate
    -greater-happiness-Penn-Princeton-research.

13. Atalay, A. S. & Meloy, M. G. (2011). "Retail Therapy: A Strategic Effort
    to Improve Mood." *Psychol. Mark.* 28, 638–659. https://doi.org/10.1002
    /mar.20404.

14. Chancellor, J. & Lyubomirsky, S. (2011). "Happiness and Thrift: When
    (Spending) Less is (Hedonically) More." *Journal of Consumer
    Psychology* 21(2), 131–138. ISSN 1057-7408. https://doi.org/10.1016
    /j.jcps.2011.02.004.

15. Van Boven, L. & Gilovich, T. (2003). "To Do or to Have? That Is the
    Question." *Journal of Personality and Social Psychology* 85(6),
    1193–1202. https://doi.org/10.1037/0022-3514.85.6.1193.

16. Lyubomirsky, S. N.D. "Sonja (Sofya) Lyubomirsky: Thwarting Hedonic
    Adaptation." https://sonjalyubomirsky.com/ (Accessed July 2023).

17. Carter, T. J. & Gilovich, T. (2010). "The Relative Relativity of Material and Experiential Purchases." *Journal of Personality and Social Psychology* 98(1), 146–159. https://doi.org/10.1037/a0017145.

18. Keinan, A., Bellezza, S. & Paharia, N. (2019). "The Symbolic Value of Time." *Current Opinion in Psychology* 26, 58–61. https://doi.org/10.1016/j.copsyc.2018.05.001.

19. Luo, Y., Hawkley, L. C., Waite, L. J. & Cacioppo, J. T. (2012). "Loneliness, Health, and Mortality in old age: A National Longitudinal Study." *Social Science & Medicine* 74(6), 907–914. https://doi.org/10.1016/j.socscimed.2011.11.028.

20. Okabe-Miyamoto, K., Walsh, L. C., Ozer, D. J. & Lyubomirsky, S. (2022). "Measuring the Experience of Social Connection within Specific Social Interactions: The Connection during Conversations Scale (CDCS)." *PLOS ONE.* https://sonjalyubomirsky.com/files/2023/06/Okabe-Miyamoto-Walsh-Ozer-Lyubomirsky-in-press.pdf.

21. The Bronfenbrenner Center for Translational Research (2021). "The Psychology of Compliments: A Nice Word Goes a Long Way." *Psychology Today.* psychologytoday.com/gb/blog/evidence-based-living/202109/the-psychology-compliments-nice-word-goes-long-way; Lyubomirsky, S., Sheldon, K. M., Schkade, D. (2005). "Pursuing Happiness: The Architecture of Sustainable Change." *Review of General Psychology,* 9, 111–131. https://doi.org/10.1037/1089-2680.9.2.111; Nelson, S. K., Della Porta, M. D., Jacobs Bao, K., Lee, H. C., Choi, I., Lyubomirsky, S. (2015). "'It's Up to You' Experimentally Manipulated Autonomy Support for Prosocial Behavior Improves Well-Being in Two Cultures Over Six Weeks." *Journal of Positive Psychology,* 10, 463–476. http://doi.org/10.1080/17439760.2014.983959.

22. Boehm, J. K., Ruberton, P. M., Lyubomirsky, S. (2017). "The Promise of Fostering Greater Happiness" *The Oxford Handbook of Positive Psychology.* https://doi.org/10.1093/oxfordhb/9780199396511.013.55.

23. Dunn, E. W., Aknin, L. B., Norton, M. I. (2008). "Spending Money on others Promotes Happiness." *Science,* 319, 1687–1688. http://doi.org/10.1126/science.1150952; Moche, H., Västfjäll, D. (2022) "To Give or to Take Money? The Effects of Choice on Prosocial Spending and Happiness." *Journal of Positive Psychology,* 17(5), 742-753. https://doi.org/10.1080/17439760.2021.1940248.

24. The University of Kansas (2019). "To Thrive, Get a Balanced Diet of Social Nutrition." today.ku.edu/2019/12/04/thrive-get-balanced-diet-social-nutrition.

25. Hall, J. A., Dominguez, J., Merolla, A. J. & Otmar, C. D. (2023). "Social Bandwidth: When and Why Are Social Interactions Energy Intensive?" *Journal of Social and Personal Relationships* 40(8), 2614–2636. https://doi.org/10.1177/02654075231154937.

26. Uziel, L. (2007). "Individual Differences in the Social Facilitation Effect: A Review and Meta-Analysis," *Journal of Research in Personality* 41(3), 579–601, ISSN 0092-6566, https://doi.org/10.1016/j.jrp.2006.06.008.
27. Hall, Jeffrey. Interview. Conducted by Amy Arthur. June 6, 2023.
28. Ibid.
29. Ibid.
30. Diener, E., Sandvik, E., Pavot, W. (2009). "Happiness Is the Frequency, Not the Intensity, of Positive versus Negative Affect." In: Diener, E. (eds). *Assessing Well-Being. Social Indicators Research Series* 39. Springer, Dordrecht. https://doi.org/10.1007/978-90-481-2354-4_10.
31. Boehm, J. K., Ruberton, P. M., Lyubomirsky, S. (2017). "The Promise of Fostering Greater Happiness." *The Oxford Handbook of Positive Psychology.* https://doi.org/10.1093/oxfordhb/9780199396511.013.55.
32. Lyubomirsky, S., Sheldon, K. M. & Schkade, D. (2005). "Pursuing Happiness: The Architecture of Sustainable Change." *Review of General Psychology* 9(2), 111–131. https://doi.org/10.1037/1089-2680.9.2.111.
33. Action for Happiness (2020). "Happiness Habits – with Sonja Lyubomirsky." youtube.com/watch?v=qYmLTG03ZDo.

Chapter Twelve—
Time and Its Limits

1. Quora (2019). "In the 400S BC, How Could Socrates Have Known the Truth of 'Beware the Barrenness of a Busy Life'? Is This A Universal Truth?" quora.com/In-the-400s-BC-how-could-Socrates-have-known-the-truth-of-Beware-the-barrenness-of-a-busy-life-Is-this-a-universal-truth.
2. Holmes, C. (2023). *Happier Hour.* Penguin Life.
3. Teuchmann, K., Totterdell, P. & Parker, S. K. (1999). "Rushed, Unhappy, and Drained: An Experience Sampling Study of Relations Between Time Pressure, Perceived Control, Mood, and Emotional Exhaustion in a Group of Accountants." *Journal of Occupational Health Psychology* 4(1), 37–54. https://doi.org/10.1037//1076-8998.4.1.37https://pubmed.ncbi.nlm.nih.gov/10100112/.
4. Holmes, C. *Happier Hour.*
5. Hofstadter, D. (1979). *Gödel, Escher, Bach: An Eternal Golden Braid.* Basic Books.
6. Burkeman, O. (2022). *Four Thousand Weeks.* Vintage.
7. Ibid.

8. Tappy L. (1996). "Thermic Effect of Food and Sympathetic Nervous System Activity in Humans." *Reproduction, Nutrition, Development* 36(4), 391–397. https://doi.org/10.1051/rnd:19960405.

9. Landsberg, L. (2012). "Core Temperature: A Forgotten Variable in Energy Expenditure and Obesity?" *Obes Rev.* 13 (Suppl 2), 97–104. https://doi.org/10.1111/j.1467-789X.2012.01040.x.

10. Holmes, C. *Happier Hour.*

11. Leclerc, F., Schmitt, B. H., Dubé, L. (1995). "Waiting Time and Decision Making: Is Time Like Money?" *Journal of Consumer Research* 22(1), 110–119. https://doi.org/10.1086/209439.

12. Attributed to Mark Twain in *Reader's Digest*, April 1934.

13. Kahneman, D. & Riis, J. (2005). "Living, and Thinking about it: Two Perspectives on Life." In: Huppert, F. A., Baylis, N. & Keverne, B. (eds). *The Science of Well-Being.* Oxford; online edn, Oxford Academic. https://doi.org/10.1093/acprof:oso/9780198567523.003.0011.

14. Arkes, H. R. & Blumer, C. (1985). "The Psychology of Sunk Cost." *Organizational Behavior and Human Decision Processes* 35(1), 124–140. ISSN 0749-5978, https://doi.org/10.1016/0749-5978(85)90049-4.

15. Kahneman, D. *Thinking, Fast and Slow.*

16. GWI (2023). "Social: Behind the Screens 2023 Trend Report."

17. Clark, J. L., Algoe, S. B. & Green, M. C. (2018). "Social Network Sites and Well-Being: The Role of Social Connection." *Current Directions in Psychological Science* 27(1), 32–37. https://doi.org/10.1177/0963721417730833.

Chapter Thirteen—
Design: The Ten Steps to a New Pace of Life

1. Milkie, M. A., Raley, S. B., Bianchi, S. M. (2009). "Taking on the Second Shift: Time Allocations and Time Pressures of U.S. Parents with Preschoolers." *Social Forces* 88(2), 487–517. https://doi.org/10.1353/sof.0.0268.

2. Carlson, D. L. (2022). "Reconceptualizing the Gendered Division of Housework: Number of Shared Tasks and Partners' Relationship Quality." *Sex Roles* 86, 528–543. https://doi.org/10.1007/s11199-022-01282-5.

Conclusion

1. Burkeman, O. *Four Thousand Weeks.*

2. Morrison, M. & Roese, N. J. (2011). "Regrets of the Typical American: Findings from a Nationally Representative Sample." *Social*

Psychological and Personality Science 2(6), 576–583. https://doi.org /10.1177/1948550611401756.

3. Gilovich, T. & Medvec, V. H. (1995). "The Experience of Regret: What, When, and Why." *Psychological Review* 102(2), 379–395. https://doi.org /10.1037/0033-295X.102.2.379.

4. Watts, A. in Burkeman, O. *Four Thousand Weeks.*

Further Reading

Chapter One—
Highs and Lows: Emotional Energy

Burnout by Gordon Parker, Gabriela Tavella, and Kerrie Eyers
Burnt Out by Selina Barker
Emotional Ignorance by Dr. Dean Burnett
From Burnout to Balance by Harriet Griffey
How Emotions Are Made by Lisa Feldman Barrett
Hysterical by Dr. Pragya Agarwal
The Happy Brain by Dr. Dean Burnett
The Stress Solution by Dr. Rangan Chatterjee
Where's My Energy Gone? by Dr. Catherine Sykes
Why Has Nobody Told Me This Before? by Dr. Julie Smith

Chapter Two—
Mind Over Matter: Mental Energy

Deep Work by Cal Newport
In Praise of Walking by Shane O'Mara
Mindwandering by Moshe Bar
Seven and a Half Lessons about the Brain by Lisa Feldman Barrett
The Stress Solution by Dr. Rangan Chatterjee
Thinking, Fast and Slow by Daniel Kahneman
What I Talk About When I Talk About Running by Haruki Murakami

Chapter Three—
In Motion: Physical Energy

Endure by Alex Hutchinson
Exercised by Daniel Lieberman
Move! by Caroline Williams
Why Calories Don't Count by Giles Yeo

Chapter Five—
Eating for Energy

Age Proof by Professor Rose Anne Kenny
Burn by Herman Ponzer
Glucose Revolution by Jessie Inchauspé
How to Build a Healthy Brain by Kimberley Wilson
How to Have the Energy by Graham Allcott and Colette Heneghan
Spoon-Fed by Tim Spector
The Food Mood Connection by Uma Naidoo
Why Calories Don't Count by Giles Yeo

Chapter Six—
Sleep in Focus

Age Proof by Rose Anne Kenny
Life Time by Professor Russell Foster
The Science of Living by Dr. Stuart Farrimond
Why We Sleep by Dr. Matthew Walker

Chapter Seven—
Rest to Recharge

Pause, Rest, Be by Octavia Raheem
Rest by Alex Soojung-Kim Pang
Rest Is Resistance by Tricia Hersey
Sacred Rest by Saundra Dalton-Smith
The Art of Rest by Claudia Hammond

Chapter Nine—
The Pacing Lifestyle

Atomic Habits by James Clear
Braintenance by Dr. Julia Ravey
Fortitude by Bruce Daisley
The Book of Boundaries by Melissa Urban
Tiny Habits by BJ Fogg
Un(Stuck) by Dr. Sophie Mort

Chapter Ten—
Small Steps to Big Goals

Braintenance by Dr. Julia Ravey
How to Change by Katy Milkman
Mindset by Dr. Carol S. Dweck

Chapter Eleven—
The Happiness of Energy

Happier Hour by Cassie Holmes
Happiness by Design by Paul Dolan
Help! by Oliver Burkeman
Solve for Happy by Mo Gawdat
The Antidote by Oliver Burkeman
The Happiness Project by Gretchen Rubin
The How of Happiness by Sonja Lyubomirsky
The Science of Happiness by Brendan Kelly

Chapter Twelve—
Time and Its Limits

Four Thousand Weeks by Oliver Burkeman
Happier Hour by Cassie Holmes
In Praise of Slow by Carl Honoré
Slow at Work by Aoife McElwain

Books About ME/CFS

Decode Your Fatigue by Alex Howard
Fighting Fatigue by Sue Pemberton and Catherine Berry
Self-Management of Long-Term Health Conditions by Kate Lorig, et al.
Through the Shadowlands by Julie Rehmeyer

Acknowledgments

The idea for a book about pacing was mine, but *Pace Yourself* belongs to so many people. I am grateful to my agent, Emma Bal, who championed this book from the very beginning. In our very first meeting—over Zoom, mid-lockdown—she was able to distill my ramblings into something concrete and showed me how pacing could help not just people with my condition, but anyone feeling exhausted, overwhelmed, and burned out.

To my editor Susanna Abbott, who has been as enthusiastic as she has been patient with me as I learned how to write a book, which, as it turns out, is no easy feat. Thank you, Susanna, for your confidence in me and in *Pace Yourself*. Thanks also to my US editor, Liz Gassman, whose insights helped provide missing pieces that I'd never have found on my own. I am indebted to the copy editors and proofreaders, including Victoria Denne and Michelle Griffin, and to the marketing and publicity teams, led by Flora Willis and Grace Harrison.

I am thankful to the many scientists and experts who spoke to me during my research, including Oliver Burkeman, Dean Burnett, Bruce Daisley, Telli Davoodi, Russell Foster, Gavin Francis, Sandro Galea, Ellen Goudsmit, Jeffrey Hall, Claudia Hammond, Hal Hershfield, Alex Howard, Alex Hutchinson, Tim Lomas, Julia Newton, Shane O'Mara, Julia Ravey, Alex Soojung-Kim Pang, and Giles Yeo.

I think this book has always been in me, growing and evolving as I learned more about my own energy and fatigue in the years following my diagnosis of ME/CFS. I am grateful to the people who have supported me in those years and beyond, across periods of good and poor health—my mum, Janice, and stepdad, Andy; my grandma Doreen and grandpy Dennis; my dad, Dave; and my siblings: my brother, Liam; my stepbrother, Rich; and stepsister, Jess. Of course, I couldn't have written *Pace Yourself* without the love and company of Millie and Mabel. Also to my in-laws, who show unlimited kindness and support at every opportunity. My mother-in-law, Jenny, and her partner, Phil; my sister-in-law, Elspeth, and her husband, Felix. I am so glad to be part of the "Arthur Clan."

To my friends, who understood that pacing myself sometimes meant cutting our meetups short or staying in together so that I could rest.

Above all, to my husband, Rowan, without whom this book wouldn't exist—his unwavering support, his provisions of excellent meals, his reminders to "Pace yourself, Amy," when it seemed like I would never meet the deadline. Thank you for your steadiness in our life together.

About the Author

~~~~~~~~~~~~~

AMY ARTHUR is an award-winning writer and science journalist, with bylines in outlets like *Popular Science*, *BBC Science Focus*, and Live Science. After being diagnosed with ME/CFS as a teenager and on the advice of a doctor, she began using an energy management tool called "pacing" to help her manage her energy and thrive again. Pacing enabled her to go from being unable to get out of bed to being able to graduate from university, live independently, socialize, and excel at work. In an era when so many struggle to find balance and flourish, Amy is passionate about making this simple tool, which has helped her so much, accessible to everyone.

For more information about Amy and her work,
visit **www.amyarthur.co.uk**.